Poet, wri
was raised
In additio
I Know W
collection
Don't You
well as th
she read
Clinton,
request of
She lives i

ALSO BY MAYA ANGELOU

Autobiography

I Know Why the Caged Bird Sings
Gather Together in My Name
Singin' and Swingin' and Gettin' Merry Like
   Christmas
The Heart of a Woman
All God's Children Need Traveling Shoes
A Song Flung Up to Heaven

Essays

Wouldn't Take Nothing for My Journey Now
Even the Stars Look Lonesome
Letter to My Daughter

Poetry

Just Give Me a Cool Drink of Water 'fore I Diiie
Oh Pray My Wings Are Gonna Fit Me Well
And Still I Rise
Shaker, Why Don't You Sing?
I Shall Not Be Moved
On the Pulse of Morning
Phenomenal Woman
The Complete Collected Poems of
   Maya Angelou
A Brave and Startling Truth
Amazing Peace
Mother
Celebrations

Children's Books

My Painted House, My Friendly Chicken,
   and Me
Kofi and His Magic

Maya's World series

Angelina of Italy
Izak of Lapland
Mikale of Hawaii
Renée Marie of France

Picture Books

Now Sheba Sings the Song
Life Doesn't Frighten Me

Cookbook

Hallelujah! The Welcome Table

GREAT FOOD, ALL DAY LONG

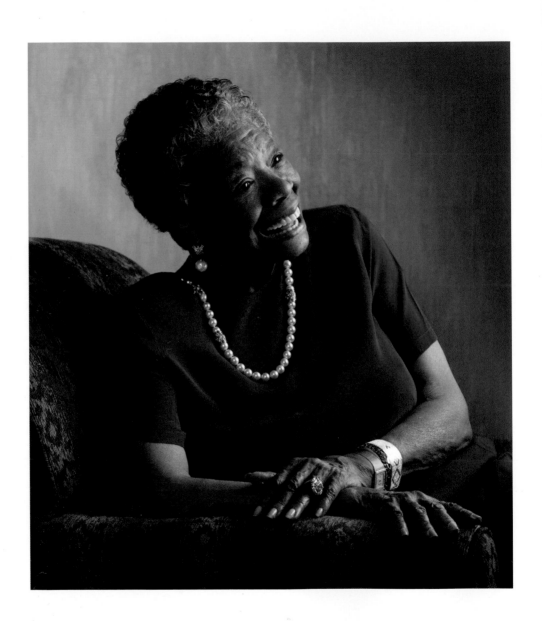

MAYA ANGELOU

GREAT FOOD, ALL DAY LONG

EAT JOYFULLY, EAT HEALTHILY

virago

VIRAGO

First published in Great Britain in 2011 by Virago Press

Copyright © Maya Angelou 2010
Photographs copyright © Sockeye Studios 2010

Interior photographs: Brian Lanker
Book design by Jo Anne Metsch

The moral right of the author has been asserted.

A CIP catalogue record for this book
is available from the British Library.

ISBN 978-1-84408-710-5

Printed and bound in China

I dedicate the ambitious intent of this book to those who would love to eat and love to lose weight at the same time.

While I cannot assure that these recipes will reduce the reader's size, I can say I have tried to offer flavors and savors which will be long remembered and always remembered with a smile of satisfaction.

Miss Dearieo, I hope this will be of use to you.

Measurements

Please note that metric, imperial and cup measurements are given for the recipes. Follow one set of measures, not a mixture, as they are not interchangeable.

All spoon measures are level unless otherwise stated. Sets of measuring spoons are available in metric and imperial for accurate measurements.

Medium eggs should be used in the recipes, except where otherwise specified.

We have included cooking temperatures for electric and gas ovens. Remember if you have a fan-assisted oven that you need to reduce the oven temperature slightly (usually by around 20 degrees) and/or adjust the cooking times. Please refer to manufacturer's guidelines for more specific information on adjusting the temperature and time for your cooker, if applicable.

Some of the recipes in this book may contain raw or lightly cooked eggs – these recipes are not recommended for babies and young children, pregant mums, the elderly and those convalescing.

Contents

Introduction

Some people buy cookbooks just to read, with no intention of trying the recipes. I hail their discipline, because it is impossible to put on weight just reading about food, even if the accompanying photographs cause the salivary glands to dance wildly in the mouth.

And there are those who want to lose weight, so they choose to read books about dieting, swearing a fierce loyalty to the books' recipes and suggestions. There are those who say they would cook if they had the time, or the skills, but since they don't, they delight in reading what serious cooks are able to create. Only a few readers buy cookbooks to really cook the recipes. If this book finds its way into the hands of bold, adventurous people, courageous enough to actually get into the kitchen and rattle the pots and pans, I will be very happy.

I started working on this book over a year ago, and in that time I have eaten from all the recipes described here. I treated myself to delicious dishes, some from my childhood and others I had encountered in travels around the world. I studied cookbooks diligently and was particularly influenced by the writers who loved food, who were gourmets but not gourmands. M.F.K. Fisher, Elizabeth David, Jessica Harris, Margaret Visser, and Jacques Pepin are among the cooks and writers whose work encouraged me.

I read that if a diner ate only a small portion of food, and waited twenty minutes, she would be surprised to find that the small amount she had consumed satisfied her hunger—that is, if the food was really savory, really tasty. Because I live alone, I knew it would be easy for me to follow that advice on portion control. If I chose to roast a chicken, I *could* plan to eat at least four meals from it. I am sure that if I had to sit at a table with my family, I would find it more challenging to eat only a little—though not impossible. The cook in the family can prepare a sumptuous meal for the family's enjoyment and still employ portion control, knowing that it's okay to return two or three hours later and, without guilt, have a little more.

I found that when I ate a few barbecued ribs and a serving of a few vegetables, I could set the rest aside and return to it later. Likewise, a piece of buttered toast and two soft-boiled eggs would successfully break my fast and fuel me for my morning's labor, or were light enough to be consumed at night without fear of indigestion and nightmares. I only noticed that I was losing weight when my clothes began to appear noticeably too large.

I put the two together and deduced that portion control was the secret to my weight loss.

Some years ago I found my health in danger because I was overweight. My doctors warned me that I was dangerously close to diabetes, hypertension, and high blood pressure. I tried any number of diets, some silly and some lugubriously serious. Nothing worked for very long. But since I enjoy food, am a good cook, and am well into my upper age group, I decided there must be a way to take the pounds off and keep them off. I made some changes and lost thirty-five pounds. I diminished my portions, and ate more frequently. The title of this book, *Great Food, All Day Long,* came from that exercise. I eat less, but more often, and the foods I create are wondrously flavorsome.

Most people on our planet live without cereal or even any knowledge that there are foods meant solely to be eaten during mornings and others for lunch and yet others for dinner. People the world over eat in the morning some of the leftovers of what they had at dinner the night before.

As I prepared to write this book, I thought of dishes that would be as good at 8:30 p.m. as they were at 8:30 a.m. I have not suggested cereal or eggs as the only breakfast foods. With my recipes you can have fried rice for breakfast, lunch, or dinner. All recipes offered in this book can be prepared and eaten all day long, beginning with a glorious chili. You can have couscous with chicken drumsticks any time of the day or night. The food should taste so good that you will be satisfied with a small portion. If you are diligent about portions, then you can snack with smaller amounts all day long.

I have not tried to cut calories by creating fat- and sugar-free dishes, although I have been careful in not overdoing those foods. I use butter, olive oil, and even lard—sparingly, but enough so that the diner can taste the flavors and be satisfied.

I hope that you will find these recipes delicious and fulfilling. I hope that portion control will come easier because of the delight that you will find in these dishes. And finally, I hope you will agree with the philosopher who said "less is more."

A BRAND-NEW LOOK AT OLD LEFTOVERS

My mother dreamed that one day we would together compose a cookbook. In her dream I would cook the entree, then she would take what was left and show how it could be prepared in such wonderful ways that the family would not have any inkling that they were being served leftovers.

We spent glorious afternoons and after-dinners imagining the wonderful dishes that could be created by adding just a few more ingredients. We imagined that a dish first served as a roasted entree would be very different if it appeared as a refried or boiled offering.

This book begins with three principal dishes and the glorious creations that can be made from them.

CROWN ROAST OF PORK

1. Preheat the oven to 190°C/375°F/Gas Mark 5.
2. Sauté the apples and prunes in the butter in a skillet over low heat.
3. After 3 minutes, remove the skillet from the heat and set the prunes aside in a separate dish. Let cool.
4. Mix the garlic, thyme, oregano, salt, and pepper with the olive oil until you have a paste. Rub the paste into the meat.
5. Place the meat in a shallow roasting pan and bake for 30 minutes.
6. Reduce the oven temperature to 160°C/325°F/Gas Mark 3 and roast for 2 hours.
7. Remove the roast from the oven once the internal temperature reads 74°C/165°F on a meat thermometer.
8. Place 1 prune on each rib and return the meat to the oven for 20 minutes.
9. Remove the meat from the oven, and put the rest of the cooled fruit into the center of the crown roast.
10. Place 1 pork chop carved from the roast and 1 tablespoon of apples onto one plate for as many servings as necessary. Refrigerate the remainder.

SERVES 8. Serving size: 1 pork chop and 1 tablespoon of apples.

3 apples, peeled, cored, and cut into large dice

16 dried pitted prunes

1 tablespoon butter

1 teaspoon granulated garlic

1 teaspoon dried thyme

1 teaspoon dried oregano

½ teaspoon salt

¼ teaspoon pepper

1½ tablespoons olive oil

2 racks, about 3.6kg/8lb, pork loin (have butcher fashion into crown roast)

If you would like to give a grand dinner party, plan to serve this crown roast of pork. Be prepared for the admiring "oohs and ahhs" that will fill the air. Remember, cooking a large amount of food does not mean that you are obliged to eat large portions.

CREAMY PORK HASH

1 medium onion, diced

2 tablespoons vegetable oil

300g/11oz can condensed
   cream of mushroom soup

75g/3oz frozen peas

75g/3oz frozen sliced carrots

115g/4oz diced cooked
   potatoes

300g/11oz cooked pork roast
   (page 5), cut into medium
   dice

½ teaspoon salt

½ teaspoon pepper

1. Sauté the onion in the vegetable oil in a skillet.
2. Add the cream of mushroom soup, peas, carrots, and potatoes.
3. Add the pork and thin the mixture with 250ml/8fl oz water.
4. Add the salt and pepper.
5. Cover the skillet and simmer for 15 minutes.
6. Serve 2 heaping tablespoons on a dinner plate. Refrigerate the remainder.

SERVES 4. Serving size: 2 heaping tablespoons.

PORK TACOS

1. Dampen each tortilla with ½ teaspoon water, and cover with a paper towel.
2. Place in a microwave oven for 10 seconds on high power, then remove. Tortillas can also be fried in oil, 1 teaspoon for each.
3. Place 2 tablespoons pork on one side of a tortilla.
4. Add 1 teaspoon cheese, 2 teaspoons lettuce, 2 teaspoons tomatoes, and 2 teaspoons salsa (and onion, if desired) to each tortilla.
5. Fold the tortillas over, covering the meat and toppings completely.

SERVES 4. Serving size: 1 taco.

4 corn tortillas

4 teaspoons vegetable oil (optional)

4 thin slices cooked pork roast (page 5), shredded by hand or using two forks

115g/4oz Monterey Jack or Gruyère cheese, grated

2–3 Little Gem lettuce, shredded

200g/7oz tomatoes, cut into large dice

450g/1lb tomato salsa

½ medium onion, thinly sliced (optional)

This is one of my favorite dishes to go back to. Within three hours, I'm almost always ready for a second taco.

PORK FRIED RICE

1. Whisk together the soy sauce and 2 tablespoons water in a small bowl until blended. Set aside.
2. In a large nonstick skillet, sauté the chopped onion, scallion tops, and garlic in 1 teaspoon of the oil on moderate heat. Fry until soft and translucent.
3. Remove the onion and garlic mixture to a bowl and set aside.
4. In the same skillet, heat ¼ teaspoon of the oil, beat the eggs, and fry until cooked through completely, tilting the pan so that the eggs evenly cover the bottom.
5. Remove the eggs from the pan and set aside. Once cooled to room temperature, cut the eggs into 1cm/½-in ribbons.
6. Heat the remaining 1 teaspoon oil in the frying pan. Add the diced pork, the rice, mushrooms, and soy mixture, and cook until heated completely. Add the onion and garlic mixture and egg ribbons. Stir thoroughly, and serve immediately.

SERVES 4. Serving size: 175g/6oz.

2 tablespoons soy sauce

1 medium onion, chopped

3 medium green scallion (spring onion) tops, chopped

2 garlic cloves, minced

2¼ teaspoons vegetable oil

2 eggs

150g/5oz cooked pork roast (page 5), cut into small dice

350g/12oz cold cooked rice

225g/8oz can sliced mushrooms, drained

PRIME RIB
The Dinner That Never Stops Giving

5-rib joint prime rib of beef

120ml/4fl oz black coffee
(optional)

Marinade

1 teaspoon granulated garlic

1 teaspoon kosher salt (sea
salt flakes)

¼ teaspoon black pepper

2 teaspoons Italian
seasoning

1 teaspoon lemon pepper

2 tablespoons olive oil

1 teaspoon French's Classic
Yellow Mustard or English
Mustard

1. For the marinade, mix together the garlic, salt, black pepper, Italian seasoning, lemon pepper, olive oil, and mustard. Stir well until the ingredients are blended into a smooth mixture.

2. Spread the marinade over the meat, covering it completely.

3. Wrap the meat loosely in aluminum foil and refrigerate overnight.

4. About 1 to 2 hours before ready to prepare, remove the meat from the refrigerator and place in a shallow roasting pan, ribs down. (The ribs will act as a rack.) Allow the roast to come to room temperature.

5. While the roast is sitting, preheat the oven to 200°C/400°F/Gas Mark 6.

6. Put the roast into the oven and cook for 20 minutes.

7. Insert a meat thermometer into the densest part of the meat. Turn the oven down to 180°C/350°F/Gas Mark 4 and cook for 1½ hours or until the temperature reaches 74°C/165°F for medium. (For well done, cook for an additional hour or until the temperature reaches 82°C/180°F; for more rare, reduce the cooking time to 1 hour or until the temperature reaches 60°C/140°F.)

8. Remove the roast from the oven and let sit for 20 minutes before carving. Carve and serve.

9. Pour the leftover drippings into a saucepan and remove the fat. Add the coffee if you like. Salt to taste. Mix well. You now have a *jus*.

10. Once finished serving, remove the remaining meat from the bones, wrap the meat and bones separately in aluminum foil, and refrigerate.

SERVES ABOUT 12. Serving size: One 115g/4oz slice.

Open-Faced Sliced Beef Sandwiches

Cooked prime rib (page 12)

475ml/16fl oz beef stock

1½ tablespoons cornstarch (cornflour)

Salt and pepper

4 thin slices sandwich bread

2 tablespoons coleslaw (optional)

1. Remove the meat from the refrigerator and slice into 4 thin slices about 25g/1oz each. Return the remaining meat to the refrigerator.
2. Prepare the gravy: Combine the beef stock and cornstarch in a bowl. Add salt and pepper to taste.
3. Pour the gravy into a skillet and add the sliced meat. Heat the meat in the gravy over low heat for 10 minutes.
4. On each of two plates, place 2 thin slices of sandwich bread. Place 1 tablespoon of gravy on each slice. Place one slice of beef on each of the 4 slices of bread. Cover with 1 to 2 more tablespoons of hot gravy.
5. Serve with coleslaw on the side, if desired.

SERVES 2. Serving size: 2 thin slices of beef on 2 slices of bread.

ROAST BEEF HASH

450g/1lb cooked prime rib
(page 12)

1 tablespoon vegetable oil

1 medium onion, diced

2 celery stalks, diced

1 white potato, peeled,
boiled, cooled to room
temperature, and diced

250ml/8fl oz beef gravy (see
page 13, gravy for
sandwiches)

Salt and pepper

3 poached eggs (optional)

1. Dice the prime rib into medium pieces.
2. Heat the oil in a skillet. Add the onion and celery, and sauté
   until translucent.
3. Add the potato and meat to the sautéed onion and celery
   and cook for 6 minutes.
4. Add the gravy to the skillet and heat for 5 minutes.
5. Season with salt and pepper to taste.
6. Serve with poached eggs, if desired.

SERVES 3 GENEROUSLY. Serving size: 3 heaping
tablespoons of hash and 1 poached egg.

Beef and Vegetable Soup

1. Put 2 litres/3½ pints water and the beef stock in a large pot.
2. Add the meat, bones, onion, bay leaf, and garlic.
3. Bring to a boil, then turn down the heat and add the carrots, potato, tomatoes, corn, and peas. Let simmer slowly for 1 hour.
4. Remove the soup from the heat, and remove the bay leaf and the bones.
5. Bring the soup to room temperature, and skim off the fat.
6. Add salt and pepper to taste, reheat and serve.

SERVES 6. Serving size: 250ml/8fl oz.

1 litre/1¾ pints beef stock

450g/1lb cooked prime rib, diced, plus reserved bones (page 12)

½ medium onion, diced

1 bay leaf

3 large garlic cloves, finely chopped

2 medium carrots, peeled and diced

1 white potato, peeled and diced

2 × 400g/14oz cans chopped tomatoes

2 × 195g/7oz cans sweetcorn

225g/8oz frozen peas

Salt and pepper

ROASTED CHICKEN

Juice of 1 lemon, plus one lemon for slicing, if desired

One roasting chicken, about 3.6kg/8lb

25g/1oz butter

½ teaspoon salt, or more if desired

½ teaspoon pepper, or more if desired

1 unpeeled Granny Smith apple, cored and cut into pieces

1 celery stalk, cut into medium-size pieces

½ cup chopped green lettuce

1. Preheat the oven to 180°C/350°F/Gas Mark 4.
2. In a small cup, mix together the lemon juice and 250ml/8fl oz water. Set the lemon aside.
3. Wash the chicken in the lemon juice mixture. Pat dry.
4. Rub the butter over the chicken.
5. Liberally salt and pepper the chicken outside and inside.
6. Place the apple and celery in the chicken cavity. Place the chicken in a roasting pan.
7. Place an extra-large piece of aluminum foil over the chicken, leaving a generous air pocket over the top of the chicken so the foil does not touch it. Crimp the ends of the foil to the sides of the pan, creating a tent.
8. Bake the chicken in the tent for 1½ hours, partially removing the tent periodically to baste with pan juices.
9. Remove the foil and reduce the oven temperature to 160°C/325°F/Gas Mark 3. Bake the chicken, uncovered, for 30 additional minutes.
10. Once the chicken is done (when the internal temperature reaches 71°C/160°F), remove the skin and slice for serving.
11. Serve with lettuce and garnish with a very thin slice of lemon, if desired.

SERVES 6. Serving size: 2 slices of breast.

A chicken breast is less caloric than chicken thighs, but one chicken thigh, skinned, can be considered a serving.

CHICKEN TETRAZZINI

1. In a large skillet, heat the oil over medium-low heat. Add the onion and sauté until translucent.
2. Add the garlic powder, white pepper, and flour to the skillet and cook for 2 minutes, stirring frequently. Be careful not to let the mixture brown.
3. Add the mushrooms, chicken, stock, cream, and salt and black pepper. Stir well to completely cover the chicken.
4. Cover and let cook for 15 to 20 minutes over low heat.
5. Bring 3 litres/5¼ pints of water to a rolling boil in a large pot. Add the pasta and let boil until cooked to desired tenderness. Drain thoroughly.
6. Serve over the cooked pasta.

SERVES 4. Serving size: 90g/3½oz pasta, ¼ of the chicken mixture.

2 tablespoons vegetable oil

1 medium onion, sliced into slivers

1 teaspoon garlic powder

½ teaspoon white pepper

2 tablespoons all-purpose (plain) flour

5 oyster mushrooms, slivered

300g/11oz roasted chicken (page 16), shredded by hand or using two forks

475ml/16floz chicken stock

120ml/4floz heavy (double) cream

1 teaspoon salt

1 teaspoon black pepper

225g/8oz dried pasta (thin spaghetti or angel hair recommended)

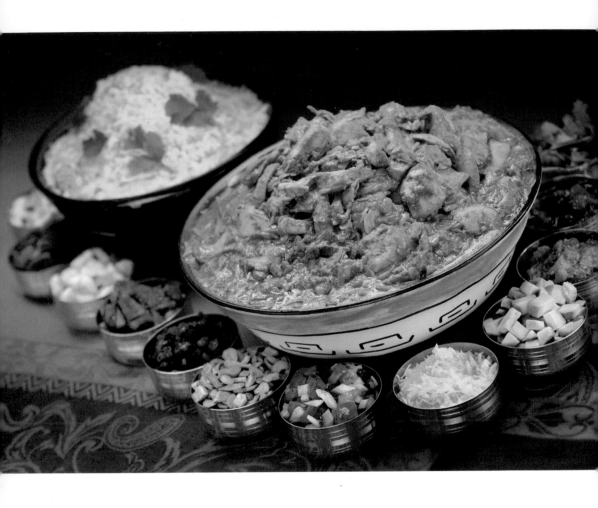

CHICKEN CURRY

1. Sauté the onion in the oil in a medium-sized skillet, until translucent; do not brown.
2. Add the curry, cumin, ginger, and bay leaf to the onion and cook for 5 minutes.
3. Add the chicken, the stock, and the salt and pepper, and cook for 10 minutes. Remove bay leaf.
4. Serve with hot white rice or rice pilaf, if desired.

SERVES 4. Serving size: 2 heaping tablespoons of curry over 175g/6oz of rice.

Relishes such as raisins, mango chutney, cashew nuts, or avocado can be offered with the curry.

1 small onion, sliced

1 tablespoon vegetable oil

4 teaspoons medium-hot curry powder

1 teaspoon ground cumin

½ teaspoon ground ginger

1 bay leaf

300g/11oz diced roasted chicken (page 16)

250ml/8fl oz chicken stock

1 teaspoon salt

1 teaspoon pepper

700g/1lb 9oz cooked white rice or rice pilaf (optional)

PALATE APPETEASERS

Teenagers may differ in ethnic, racial, cultural, and economic backgrounds—African American, White American, Asian, Latino, and Native American—but there is one area where they are alike: They all love hot dogs. The flavor of the wiener, the choice or choices of mustard, relish, ketchup, or sauerkraut may vary, but young palates are satisfied with the simple everyday hot dog.

I confess that on certain days, a similar yearning also comes over me, and I can only be satisfied with a loaded hot dog. That said, my palate has had the opportunity to develop some sophistication.

Take, for instance, moo goo gai pan. When my son, Guy, was six, we would often dine at a little Chinese restaurant in San Francisco. Their moo goo gai pan—chicken wings boiled and rolled in a batter with sesame seeds, and fried—was Guy's favorite, and because he loved it so much, I learned to make it.

I've also come to like red tripe, which is tripe cooked with red tomatoes, onion, and garlic and served over steamed white rice. I do make a very good duck liver pâté with truffles, and mustard greens with ham hocks, which can make a person cry for his grandmother, but . . . back to the hot dog.

When I make a chili, I always put about a quart away in the freezer in half-cup portions. Weeks or months later, long after the chili has first been served, I will get a hot dog bun, a Hebrew National wiener, prick it with a fork, broil it for a few minutes, and split it. Then I heat up the chili, put one half of the split hot dog on the bottom piece of bun, and put one heaping tablespoon of chili on the hot dog. I put away the other half for later. Next, I scatter a teaspoon of diced raw onion onto that concoction, then open an ice-cold beer and pour half of it into an ice-cold mug.

At that moment I will not only not answer the telephone, I will not respond, even if my name is called by someone who knows me well.

Chili Guy

1. Sauté the onion and garlic in the vegetable oil in a medium-sized heavy pot until translucent.
2. Add the ground beef and pork. Cook until the meat is cooked all the way through, about 15 minutes, stirring frequently.
3. Add the oregano, thyme, sage, cardamom, chili powder, salt, black pepper, and cayenne pepper and cook for 3 more minutes.
4. Add the tomatoes and tomato paste, and stir until all the ingredients are mixed together well. Cover and cook over medium heat for 20 minutes.
5. Add the beef stock or water, cornmeal, and rinsed pinto beans, if desired, and stir.
6. Cover and reduce the heat, and simmer for 1 hour.

SERVES 4 TO 6. Serving size: 150g/5oz of chili over 90g/3½oz of rice.

This recipe would be sufficient for 4 to 6 hearty diners. It also serves a party very well. If your party is larger, double or triple the recipe as needed. If you have leftovers, let them cool, place in zippered bags, and freeze to be used at a later date (with a hot dog!).

1 medium onion, chopped

2 garlic cloves, chopped

4 tablespoons vegetable oil

450g/1lb extra-lean ground (minced) beef

150g/5oz ground (minced) pork

½ teaspoon dried oregano

½ teaspoon dried thyme

½ teaspoon dried sage

¼ teaspoon ground cardamom

2 tablespoons chili powder

¼ teaspoon salt

⅛ teaspoon black pepper

¼ teaspoon cayenne pepper

200g/7oz canned chopped tomatoes

115g/4oz tomato paste (purée)

475ml/16floz beef stock or water

3 teaspoons cornmeal

400g/14oz can pinto beans, drained and rinsed (optional)

Steamed rice (optional)

Santa Fe Chili with Meat

900g/2lb chuck or braising steak, cut into 4cm/1½-in cubes

50g/2oz all-purpose (plain) flour

2 large onions, chopped

3 garlic cloves, finely chopped or crushed

120ml/4fl oz olive oil or other vegetable oil

Red Chile Sauce (page 29; optional)

2 tablespoons finely chopped fresh cilantro (coriander)

2 teaspoons ground cumin

¼ teaspoon ground cloves

1 teaspoon crushed dried oregano

1½ teaspoons dried rosemary

1½ teaspoons dried tarragon

2 × 800g/1¾lb cans whole tomatoes and their liquid

475ml/16fl oz homemade chicken stock or one 400g/14oz can low-sodium chicken or beef stock

Steamed rice

1. Sprinkle the beef with the flour in a bowl and mix together. Set aside.
2. In a 6- to 8-litre/11–14 pint pot, cook the onions and garlic in the oil over medium heat, stirring often, until the onions are soft, about 10 minutes.
3. Add the meat mixture and Red Chile Sauce (if desired) to the pot. Cook, stirring constantly, until the meat begins to brown, about 5 minutes.
4. Add the cilantro, cumin, cloves, oregano, rosemary, tarragon, tomatoes and their liquid, and stock. Simmer, uncovered, until the meat is very tender, about 1 hour, stirring often.

SERVES 4 TO 6. Serving size: 75g/3oz of chili over 90g/3½oz of rice.

For a more flavorful dish, cook and refrigerate for up to 2 days, and reheat before serving. Or place in zippered bags and freeze to be used with a hot dog at a later date. And for a spicier kick, add more Red Chile Sauce (page 29) to taste.

Red Chile Sauce

1. Stem and seed the chiles and combine with 750ml/1¼pints water in a 2½- to 3-litre/4½–5½pint pot.
2. Cover and simmer over medium-low heat until the chiles are very soft, about 30 minutes.
3. Remove the chiles from the pan and place them in a blender, saving the cooking water.
4. Puree the chiles, adding cooking water as needed, until you have a very smooth mixture, about 3 minutes.
5. Pour the sauce through a fine strainer, rubbing firmly, into a container. Discard the residue.
6. Add the sauce to chili or other dishes as desired.

115g/4oz dried whole red chiles (New Mexico or Anaheim chiles work best)

Spicy Barbecued Spareribs

1 teaspoon salt

½ teaspoon pepper

900g/2lb baby back
   spareribs, cut into 3- or
   4-rib serving pieces

250ml/8fl oz chicken stock

Barbecue Sauce

120ml/4fl oz vinegar

2 tablespoons honey

75ml/2½fl oz tomato ketchup

1 teaspoon powdered
   mustard

½ teaspoon paprika

Dash of hot pepper sauce

1 garlic clove, finely chopped

½ teaspoon salt

¼ teaspoon black pepper

1. Preheat the oven to 180°C/350°F/Gas Mark 4.
2. Stir together 1 teaspoon salt and ½ teaspoon pepper. Sprinkle over the spareribs and rub in thoroughly. Place the coated ribs in a shallow roasting pan.
3. Pour the chicken stock over the ribs and place the ribs in the oven. Cook for 1½ hours or until tender.
4. Meanwhile, prepare the barbecue sauce. Mix together the vinegar, honey, ketchup, mustard, paprika, hot pepper sauce, garlic, ½ teaspoon salt and ¼ teaspoon pepper in a small saucepan. Simmer over low heat for 15 minutes.
5. Remove the spareribs from the oven and place them in a grill pan. Brush the spareribs with the barbecue sauce and return to the oven on the lowest rack. Set the oven to low grill, and grill the spareribs for 30 minutes, brushing frequently with the sauce. To tell when they're done, pierce the meat between the bones with a fork. If the fork comes out easily, the meat is done.

SERVES 4. Serving size: 225g/8oz of ribs.

IS VARIETY FINE CUISINE?

Many years ago I was invited to be a distinguished visiting professor at Wichita State University. I taught there for four weeks while staying with family friends.

My hosts, Dr. and Mrs. George Rogers, had two daughters and the first microwave I had ever seen. The daughters were very clever teenagers, who cooked everything they could find in the microwave oven.

I elected to cook some special dishes for the family. I prepared a beef bourguignonne one night, and a beef stroganoff a few days later. On a Sunday I cooked curried lamb and served it with mango chutney, cucumber, cashew nuts, raisins, and diced tomatoes.

While the adults enjoyed my creations, the young ladies could barely choke them down.

My husband, Paul, visited from California for a weekend, and he offered to cook his version of a London grill. He fried steak, liver, bacon, a beef kidney, and pounds of sliced onions in butter. The Rogers girls loved the fried dinner. They ate bites of everything and then as we sat around the table, they said, "We know who the real cook is in your family, Auntie Maya. Your meats were okay, but the gravies were horrible, and it took you so long to cook everything. Uncle Paul has come and within an hour he has us all sitting at the table eating a gourmet dinner."

I kicked Paul under the table.

This is a great meal to serve a large party of carnivores. There is something within this mélange to satisfy any and every palate, and since the meats are sliced in strips 1 inch thick and 2 inches long, everyone can sample everything without overeating.

When I was young, my mother would watch young women pay our butcher sixteen dollars for two half-pound cuts of filet mignon. She then would pay the butcher thirty-two dollars for the whole beef loin, from which she could get twelve hearty steaks and eight to ten cuts of filet mignon. I do the same to this day, and have found that using filet mignon instead of top sirloin adds a touch of sophistication—and succulence—to my London grill.

Mixed London Grill

1. Wash the kidney halves and remove all the veins and fat.
2. Soak in water with ½ teaspoon of the salt for 1 hour and pat dry.
3. While the kidney is soaking, season the bratwurst, lamb chops, pork loin, beef, veal, and livers with pepper and the remaining 1½ teaspoons salt.
4. Grill the pork loin in a grill pan on top of the stove until cooked all the way through. Then grill the kidney, bratwurst, lamb, beef, veal, and liver until medium done. Set aside in a warming dish.
5. In a large skillet, fry the bacon until crispy, turning frequently. Remove the bacon and add to the dish with the grilled meats.
6. Return the skillet to the stove, and fry the onions in the oil.
7. Mix all the meats and the onions together and put over low heat for 5 minutes or until all are warm and cooked through.
8. Serve on a warm platter with a 2.5cm/1-in-thick slice of grilled or toasted sourdough bread.

SERVES 6. Serving size: 1 spoonful of onions, 1 forkful of each meat, 1 slice of bacon, and ½ slice toasted bread. Be careful with portions, and be discreet. You can always go back.

1 lamb or veal kidney, halved

2 teaspoons salt

1 whole bratwurst or other sausage

2 lamb chops

2 thin slices pork loin

900g/2lb sirloin steak, sliced

900g/2lb veal cutlets, sliced

900g/2lb calves' livers, sliced

¼ teaspoon pepper

8 rashers bacon

225g/8oz onions, sliced

2 tablespoons vegetable oil

Toasted sourdough bread

Shepherd's Pie

115g/4oz streaky bacon, finely chopped

450g/1lb ground (minced) beef

1 garlic clove, chopped

2 shallots, chopped

1 medium onion, chopped

1 tablespoon chopped fresh parsley

2 tablespoons tomato paste (purée)

2 tablespoons dry white wine

1 teaspoon salt

½ teaspoon pepper

800g/1¾lb potatoes, peeled and cubed

3¼ tablespoons butter, cut into small pieces

⅛ teaspoon ground nutmeg (optional)

50g/2oz cheddar cheese, grated

This dish is especially filling and satisfying when served with a romaine lettuce salad with vinaigrette.

1. In a large skillet set over high heat, cook the bacon until crisp and remove to paper towels to drain.
2. Fry the beef in the bacon fat.
3. Add to the beef the garlic, shallots, onion, parsley, tomato paste, wine, ½ teaspoon of the salt and ¼ teaspoon of the pepper.
4. Simmer over low heat, partially covered, for 30 minutes, stirring occasionally.
5. While the beef is simmering, boil the potatoes in water in a medium-sized saucepan with the remaining ½ teaspoon salt until tender, about 2 minutes.
6. Drain the potatoes and mash, mixing in 2 tablespoons of the butter.
7. Season with the remaining ¼ teaspoon pepper, and the nutmeg, if desired.
8. Preheat the oven to 230°C/450°F/Gas Mark 8. Use ¼ tablespoon of the butter to coat the bottom and sides of a shallow 23 × 32cm/9 × 13-inch casserole or baking dish.

9. Spread a layer of potatoes on the bottom of the dish. Place all of the meat mixture and bacon on top of the potato layer, and cover with the remaining potatoes.
10. Sprinkle with the cheddar cheese and dot with the remaining 1 tablespoon butter.
11. Bake for 20 minutes or until the cheese is melted and lightly browned and the dish is hot throughout.

SERVES 6 OR 7. **Serving size: 3 tablespoons.**

Original Joe's Sausage, Eggs, and Greens

900g/2lb red or green Swiss chard

2 tablespoons vegetable oil

450g/1lb mild Italian sausage, casings removed

2 large onions, finely chopped

2 garlic cloves, finely chopped

225g/8oz mushrooms, sliced

¼ teaspoon ground nutmeg

¼ teaspoon pepper

¼ teaspoon dried oregano

475ml/16fl oz beef stock

6 large eggs

Salt

115g/4oz Monterey Jack or Gruyère cheese, grated

1. Rinse the greens well. Cut the chard leaves into thin shreds; thinly slice the stems. You should have about 5 cups, lightly packed. Set the greens aside.
2. Place a wok or 30- to 35cm/12- to 14-inch skillet over high heat. Add the oil.
3. Crumble the sausage into the pan, stirring frequently until the meat is well browned, about 10 minutes.
4. Add the onions, garlic, mushrooms, nutmeg, pepper, and oregano. Stir often, until the onions are soft.
5. Add the beef stock.
6. Stir in the greens, a portion at a time, until all the greens are in the pan and just wilted, 10 minutes.
7. Beat the eggs lightly in a bowl. Add the eggs to the pan and stir over low heat just until softly set.
8. Season to taste with salt.
9. Transfer to a warm serving dish and sprinkle with the cheese.

SERVES 6 OR MORE. Serving size: 1 cup.

Pytt I Panna
Swedish Hash

1. In a large skillet, heat 3 tablespoons of the oil over medium heat. Add the onions and sauté until soft and golden, about 5 minutes.
2. Using a slotted spoon, transfer the onions to a hot plate, leaving as much oil as possible in the skillet.
3. Return the skillet to the heat and brown the potatoes for 4 minutes. Using the slotted spoon, transfer the potatoes to the plate with the onions, again leaving as much oil as possible in the skillet.
4. Return the skillet to the heat and warm the meat for approximately 3 minutes. Return the onions and potatoes to the skillet and mix thoroughly with the meat.
5. Season with the salt and pepper and heat thoroughly for 2 minutes.
6. In a separate frying pan, add the remaining ½ tablespoon oil, and fry the eggs.
7. Serve the hash on the hot plate, garnished with the fried eggs and sliced cucumber pickles.

SERVES 4. Serving size: 1 cup of hash with 1 egg.

3½ tablespoons vegetable oil

3 medium onions, diced

350g/12oz cooked potatoes, peeled and diced

300g/11oz leftover cooked beef, diced

½ teaspoon salt

¼ teaspoon pepper

4 large eggs

Cucumber (dill) pickles, sliced

Meat Loaf

1. Sauté the onion and celery in the oil until translucent. Add the breadcrumbs, thyme, basil, and red wine. Remove from the heat and allow to cool for 15 minutes.
2. In a large bowl, combine the cooled mixture with the beef, veal, and pork, mixing well.
3. In a separate bowl, beat together the milk, egg, beef stock, salt, and pepper. Pour into the meat and combine. Cover with aluminum foil and refrigerate for 2 hours.
4. Preheat the oven to 190°C/375°F/Gas Mark 5.
5. Remove the meat from the refrigerator and place in a loaf pan, packing firmly.
6. Bake for 1 hour and 20 minutes.
7. Spread the ketchup over the meat loaf and return the loaf to the oven for 15 minutes.

SERVES 6. Serving size: One 115g/4oz slice.

2 tablespoons finely chopped onion

50g/2oz very finely chopped celery

2 tablespoons vegetable oil

90g/3½oz dried breadcrumbs

¼ teaspoon dried thyme

¼ teaspoon dried basil

120ml/4fl oz red wine

500g/1¼lb lean ground (minced) beef

225g/8oz veal, ground (minced)

115g/4oz lean pork, ground (minced)

120ml/4fl oz milk

1 egg

250ml/8fl oz beef stock

1 teaspoon salt

¼ teaspoon pepper

3 tablespoons tomato ketchup

TIP

Shop Well and Cook Well

It is wise for a cook to spend serious money on heavy pots. The same goes for good knives. It is wise for a cook to make friends in a local kitchen store, where there will be news about cooking classes and a good produce market, and where knives can be sharpened.

Sweet-and-Sour Meatballs

1. Combine the breadcrumbs, onion, salt, and pepper with 350ml/12fl oz water in a large bowl. Let stand for 5 to 10 minutes.
2. Lightly beat the eggs in a separate small bowl. Add the eggs, ground beef, pork, and tomato sauce to the breadcrumb mixture. Mix well.
3. Shape into small balls (20 to 30).
4. Preheat the oven to 180°C/350°F/Gas Mark 4.
5. Heat the oil in a large skillet. Brown the meatballs in the oil. Remove the meatballs to a roasting pan and pour out the fat in the skillet.
6. Combine 350ml/12fl oz water and the stock in the skillet. Stir and pour over the meatballs.
7. Cover the roasting pan with aluminum foil and bake for about 20 minutes.
8. Meanwhile prepare the sweet-and-sour sauce. In a large saucepan, combine 1 litre/1¾ pints water, the vinegar, brown sugar, and soy sauce and bring to a boil.
9. Thicken with the cornstarch mixed with 50ml/2fl oz cold water and cook until the sauce is thick and clear.
10. Remove the meatballs from the oven and pour the sweet-and-sour sauce over them. Return them to the oven for 10 minutes.

SERVES 7 OR 8. Serving size: 3 small meatballs with sauce over 90g/3½oz cooked rice.

75g/3oz fine dried breadcrumbs

1 tablespoon instant minced onion

½ teaspoon salt

¼ teaspoon pepper

3 eggs

900g/2lb ground (minced) beef

450g/1lb pork sausagemeat

300ml/½ pint tomato sauce

2 tablespoons vegetable oil

250ml/8fl oz beef stock

Sweet-and-Sour Sauce

175ml/6fl oz apple cider vinegar

200g/7oz firmly packed light brown sugar

4 tablespoons soy sauce

65g/2½oz cornstarch (cornflour)

WAKING UP TASTE BUDS

Taste buds are particular and unique to each person. I accept the phrase "It calls for an acquired taste," which allows that upon first meeting a comestible and hating it, over time one can become not only used to it, but desirous of it. I have come to like, and even love, foods that at first sight, I wished to never taste again, see, or have their names spoken in my vicinity.

For instance, I thought that eggplant was a waste not only of the chef's time, but even wondered if the Creator could not have used time to better results. My lack of appreciation was the result of eating an eggplant dish called "poor man's caviar." When I had the good fortune to eat ratatouille, and eggplant Parmesan, I came under the spell of eggplant and I expect to be mesmerized by that vegetable my life long.

There are some dishes that have not caught my fancy yet, but I will not close the door and say I will never order them and enjoy their flavors. In today's world, with the general concern about starvation and obesity, I have discovered that overeating can be countered by making the food savory and by eating small portions throughout the day and evening. The eater will be pleased with quality rather than quantity.

Eggplant Parmesan

1. Sprinkle the salt onto the eggplant in a colander placed in the sink. Let drain for 1 hour. Rinse and pat dry.
2. Heat the olive oil in a skillet.
3. Sprinkle the granulated garlic on the eggplant slices. Dip each slice into the breadcrumbs and fry in the hot skillet for 3 minutes on each side.
4. Remove to paper towels to absorb unnecessary oil.
5. Preheat the oven to 180°C/350°F/Gas Mark 4.
6. Place the eggplant in an oiled baking pan.
7. Spread a teaspoon of tomato sauce onto each eggplant slice and sprinkle with the cheese, covering completely.
8. Bake for 20 minutes or until the cheese is melted and lightly browned. Serve immediately.

SERVES 4 OR 5. Serving size: 2 slices of eggplant.

2 teaspoons salt

1 large eggplant (aubergine), cut horizontally into 1cm/½-in slices

3 tablespoons olive oil

2 teaspoons granulated garlic

50g/2oz seasoned breadcrumbs

300g/11oz tomato sauce

75g/3oz Parmesan cheese, grated

Braised Lamb with White Beans

225g/8oz dried white beans, soaked overnight in cold water to cover

1 bouquet garni (1 sprig each thyme and parsley, 1 bay leaf, and 6 cloves tied in a square of cheesecloth)

¾ medium onion, chopped

¾ medium carrot, chopped

675g/1½lb lean lamb shoulder

½ teaspoon salt

¼ teaspoon pepper

¼ teaspoon sugar

2 tablespoons all-purpose (plain) flour

1½ tablespoons vegetable oil

350ml/12fl oz dry white wine

¾ tablespoon tomato paste (purée)

1½ ripe tomatoes, quartered

3 garlic cloves, crushed

Italian bread (optional)

1. Drain the water from the beans.
2. Cover the beans, bouquet garni, onion, and carrot completely with water in a large, heavy-bottomed saucepan. Cover and bring to a boil, then reduce the heat to low and simmer for 1½ hours.
3. Meanwhile, put the lamb in a large bowl and sprinkle with the salt, pepper, sugar, and flour.
4. Heat the oil in a large skillet, add the seasoned lamb, and brown it over medium heat.
5. Add the beans, bouquet garni, onion, and carrot and their liquid to the lamb.
6. Add the white wine, tomato paste, tomatoes, and garlic. Bring to a boil.
7. Cover and simmer until the liquid has been reduced and all the ingredients are tender.
8. Discard the bouquet garni. Carve the lamb into 1cm/½in thick slices and serve with the beans.

SERVES: 6 TO 8. Serving size: 1 slice lamb, 4 tablespoons beans and 1 piece of hot Italian bread, if desired.

Club Steaks with Parsley Butter

4 individual club (rib-eye)
  steaks, about 150g/5oz
  each

1 tablespoon vegetable oil

½ teaspoon kosher salt (sea
  salt flakes)

50ml/2fl oz dry red wine

175ml/6fl oz beef stock

1 tablespoon butter

½ teaspoon whole black
  peppercorns

Parsley Butter

2 tablespoons chopped fresh
  parsley

1 tablespoon butter

This is also delicious
cold or sliced into salad
greens.

1. Trim any fat from the steaks.
2. Heat the oil in a large skillet over medium heat and sear the
   steaks in the hot oil, frying for 3 to 4 minutes on each side.
3. Remove the steaks to a warm platter and sprinkle with the
   salt.
4. Quickly pour the wine into the hot skillet; let it sizzle and
   reduce by more than half, about 2 minutes.
5. Add the beef stock and continue to boil until reduced to
   about 75ml/2½fl oz. Add the butter and peppercorns, stirring until the butter is melted.
6. Remove the peppercorns to a paper towel. Using a mallet
   or heavy pan, crack the peppercorns and return them to the
   skillet. Stir well.
7. Prepare the parsley butter: In a food processor, blend
   together the parsley and butter until smooth.
8. Spoon the sauce over the steaks and serve with 1 teaspoon
   of parsley butter each.

SERVES 4. Serving size: 1 steak and green salad.

TIP

Flavored Butters

Herb Butter

25g/1oz fresh basil, or
25g/1oz fresh thyme, or
25g/1oz fresh oregano, or
25g/1oz fresh rosemary.
115g/4oz butter or margarine, at room temperature

1. Wash the herb of your choice thoroughly and dry thoroughly. Strip the leaves from the stems and very finely chop.
2. Mix the herbs with the soft butter and place the butter on greaseproof paper.
3. Roll the butter into a log and place the log packet in aluminum foil. Roll tightly and place in the refrigerator.

MAKES 115g/4oz

Garlic-Cilantro Butter

115g/4oz butter or margarine, at room temperature
25g/1oz fresh cilantro (coriander) leaves, chopped
2 garlic cloves, finely chopped or crushed

Using a food processor, mix the ingredients together.

MAKES 115g/4oz

These flavored butters can be prepared using other herbs, like dill and marjoram. If you want to serve butter over individual steaks, unwrap the log and cut round pats of butter. Replace the roll in the refrigerator and put 1 pat over each steak as it is served.

Oxtail Stew

1 tablespoon vegetable oil

900g/2lb oxtail, cut into 5cm/2-in pieces

2 to 3 tablespoons all-purpose (plain) flour

1 celery stalk, coarsely chopped

½ bay leaf

½ teaspoon dried thyme

3 garlic cloves

475ml/16fl oz boiling water

6 small carrots, peeled

1 tablespoon finely chopped fresh parsley

½ teaspoon salt

¼ teaspoon pepper

1. Heat the oil in a large heavy skillet.
2. Dredge the oxtail in the flour in a bowl, and place in the skillet. Stir constantly over brisk heat until the meat is seared, about 15 minutes.
3. Add the celery, bay leaf, thyme, and garlic, stirring constantly until brown.
4. Stir in the boiling water, reduce the heat, cover, and simmer for 1½ hours.
5. Add the carrots and parsley and continue simmering for 1½ additional hours or until the meat is tender. Remove bay leaf. Add the salt and pepper.

SERVES 6 TO 8. Serving size: 1 piece of oxtail and 2 tablespoons of gravy.

Scallops of Turkey Breast

1. Slice the turkey breast into 8 slices (escalopes or scallops).
2. Pat the scallops dry and dust with the flour, well seasoned with the salt and pepper.
3. Place between pieces of greaseproof paper and pound each scallop two or three times with a rolling pin.
4. Heat the butter and oil to sizzling in a large skillet. Brown the scallops three or four at a time to avoid crowding, turning each when brown.
5. Return all the scallops to the pan and cook for 5 minutes. Remove, set aside, and cover to keep warm.
6. In the same pan, cook the shallots until brown, add the wine, and cook down quickly, scraping up the braised bits.
7. Add the milk and cook the mixture down to a syrupy thickness, creating a sauce.
8. Reduce the heat and return the scallops to the pan with the sauce. (If the sauce is too thick, thin with the chicken stock, adding a little at a time to obtain the desired consistency.)
9. Sprinkle the turkey with the toasted sesame seeds and serve.

SERVES 8. Serving size: 1 scallop.

1.8kg/4lb turkey breast

25g/1oz all-purpose (plain) flour

½ teaspoon salt

¼ teaspoon pepper

1 tablespoon butter

2 tablespoons vegetable oil

2 tablespoons finely chopped shallots or scallions (spring onions)

50ml/2fl oz dry white wine

120ml/4fl oz skim milk

75ml/2½fl oz chicken stock (optional)

4 tablespoons sesame seeds, toasted

Cabbage Rolls with Sauerkraut and Pork

1. Bring 1 litre/1¾ pints of water to a boil with the salt in a medium saucepan.
2. Add the cabbage leaves and boil for 4 to 7 minutes. Drain and dry on paper towels.
3. In a large skillet, sauté the chorizo and onion until the onion is translucent. Remove from the heat and let cool.
4. Season the meat mixture with the pepper and mix with the rice. Place 2 tablespoons of the meat mixture in each cabbage leaf. Roll the leaves and secure with toothpicks or poultry skewers. Set aside.
5. In a clean skillet, layer the sauerkraut and cabbage rolls, beginning and ending with the sauerkraut.
6. Add 1 litre/1¾ pints water and simmer for 35 minutes, adding more water if needed.
7. Sprinkle with paprika and serve each roll with a dollop of sour cream.

¼ teaspoon salt

6 large cabbage leaves

225g/8oz fresh chorizo pork sausage (if dried, remove casings)

1½ tablespoons finely chopped onion

¼ teaspoon pepper

275g/10oz cooked rice

200g/7oz sauerkraut, thoroughly washed

Paprika

225g/8oz sour cream

SERVES 6. Serving size: 1 cabbage roll, with a spoonful of sauerkraut.

FILLING AND FULFILLING

hildhood stories, fairy tales, and myths have told us that that which we seek may be found at the bottom of fountains, or by rubbing magic lamps, or at the end of rainbows. Princesses—and what girl is not one—have been led to think that they might, just might, kiss frogs and be rewarded by finding handsome princes in attendance.

I have noticed that many people eat long after they are filled. I think they are searching in their plates not for a myth, but for a taste, which seems to elude them. If a person's taste buds are really calling for a prime rib of beef or a crispy brown pork chop, stewed chicken will not satisfy. So the diner will have another piece of chicken and another piece of bread and some more potatoes, searching in vain for the flavor that is missing.

You will note in this cookbook that from time to time I will deliver philosophical announcements. I don't think there is an excuse for that. However, there is an explanation.

At one time, I described myself as a cook, a driver, and a writer. I no longer drive, but I do still write and I do still cook. And having reached the delicious age of eighty-one, I realize that I have been feeding other people and eating for a long time. I have been cooking nearly all my life, so I have developed some philosophies. Maybe some are high flown, but at least I have tested them and found them to the point. I believe that a bowl of savory clear soup served with a corn stick or a slice of irresistible corn bread can be filling and fulfilling. I believe if you will try these dishes together and wait two or three hours before another serving, you will be fulfilled.

Pork Pie

1. Combine the pork, nutmeg, mace, cornstarch, salt and pepper, and 250ml/8fl oz water in a large bowl. Blend thoroughly with a wooden spoon. Transfer to a skillet and simmer, covered, for 30 minutes, stirring frequently. Once the meat is thoroughly cooked, remove from the heat and set aside to cool.
2. Preheat the oven to 220°C/425°F/Gas Mark 7.
3. Pour the meat mixture into the bottom crust in a pie pan. Cover with the remaining pastry and seal the edges with water.
4. Mix the egg and 120ml/4fl oz water in a cup. Brush the egg wash over the pastry.
5. Prick the sealed pie with a fork to allow steam to escape during baking. Place the pie in the oven and bake for 10 minutes.
6. Reduce the heat to 180°C/350°F/Gas Mark 4 and bake for 35 minutes longer or until the top is brown.

SERVES 6. Serving size: 1 slice. (Slice the pie into 6 pieces.)

450g/1lb lean ground (minced) pork
¼ teaspoon ground nutmeg
⅛ teaspoon ground mace
2 teaspoons cornstarch (cornflour)
1 teaspoon salt
½ teaspoon pepper
2 20cm/8in piecrusts (pastry cases), defrosted if frozen
1 egg

TIP

Time Yourself

Plan your meal carefully. If you are cooking meat, remember it will take longer than vegetables, and some vegetables will cook before others. Do not start every dish at the same time.

Mixed-Up Tamale Pie

1. Lightly coat a medium casserole dish with 1 teaspoon of the oil and set aside.
2. Heat the remaining oil in a large skillet. Add the ground beef, onion, tomatoes, garlic, tomato sauce, salt, and pepper. Cover and simmer for 20 minutes.
3. Add the corn, taco sauce, chili powder, and olives.
4. Mix together the cornmeal and 250ml/8fl oz water in a bowl until smooth. Pour into the skillet with the meat. Stir until all the ingredients are thoroughly combined.
5. Pour into the prepared baking dish and sprinkle the cheese on top.
6. Bake for 50 minutes to 1 hour, until lightly browned on top.

SERVES 6. Serving size: 3 heaping tablespoons. Serve with lettuce salad.

3 tablespoons vegetable oil

450g/1lb ground (minced) beef

1 medium onion, chopped

One 400g/14oz can crushed tomatoes

2 garlic cloves, minced

225g/8oz tomato pasta sauce

¼ teaspoon salt

¼ teaspoon pepper

400g/14oz tinned sweetcorn

150g/5oz taco sauce or tomato sauce with chili

2 teaspoons chili powder

90g/3½oz pitted black olives

6 tablespoons yellow cornmeal

115g/4oz diced sharp cheddar cheese

Veal Chops Supreme

½ teaspoon salt

¼ teaspoon pepper

50g/2oz all-purpose (plain) flour

Four 4cm/1½in-thick veal chops

2 tablespoons vegetable oil

225g/8oz sour cream

1. Preheat the oven to 180°C/350°F/Gas Mark 4.
2. Whisk together the salt, pepper, and flour in a bowl. Coat the veal chops lightly in the seasoned flour.
3. Heat the oil in a large skillet. Add the chops and cook until brown.
4. Remove the chops and place in a shallow baking dish.
5. Add 250ml/8fl oz hot water to the skillet and stir in half of the sour cream until well blended. Pour enough over the chops to half cover them.
6. Bake, covered, for 1 hour.
7. Remove the chops from the oven. Stir the remaining sour cream into the mixture in the skillet and pour over the chops.
8. Cut each chop in half and serve.

SERVES 6 TO 8. Serving size: ½ chop with 1 portion of roasted vegetables (page 96).

Pollo in Salsa

1. Season the chicken with ½ teaspoon of the salt and ¼ teaspoon of the pepper. Dredge in flour.
2. Heat the oil in a large skillet. Add the chicken and brown on all sides.
3. Remove the chicken onto paper towels.
4. Return the skillet to the heat and brown the onion and garlic in any remaining oil. Add the chili powder, remaining salt and pepper, the bay leaves, and cumin.
5. Mash the tomatoes and cinnamon and add to the skillet. Add the boiling water and simmer for 20 minutes.
6. Return the chicken to the skillet and cook until tender, turning occasionally, about 30 minutes. Add more water if necessary to reach the cook's desired thickness. Remove bay leaves before serving.

SERVES 6 TO 8. Serving size: 1 piece of chicken.

1 chicken, cut up
1 teaspoon salt
½ teaspoon pepper
50g/2oz all-purpose (plain) flour
4 tablespoons vegetable oil
1 medium onion, chopped
2 garlic cloves, chopped
⅛ to ½ teaspoon chili powder
2 bay leaves
½ teaspoon ground cumin
800g/1¾lb can whole tomatoes
1 cinnamon stick
475ml/16fl oz boiling water

Puchero and Corn Bread

675g/1½lb beef brisket

450g/1lb beef short ribs

115g/4oz all-purpose (plain)
flour

2 tablespoons vegetable oil

450g/1lb kielbasa (Polish
sausage)

115g/4oz salt pork, sliced

2 garlic cloves, finely
chopped

1 teaspoon dried basil

1 teaspoon ground cumin

1 teaspoon dried thyme

1 teaspoon dried rosemary

2 celery stalks, chopped

1 medium onion, chopped

½ teaspoon salt

¼ teaspoon pepper

475ml/16fl oz beef stock

225g/8oz can chickpeas,
drained

2 medium carrots, peeled
and cut into large dice

2 sweet potatoes, peeled and
cut into large dice

225g/8oz pumpkin, cut into
large dice

175g/6oz frozen corn

All Day and All Night Corn
Bread (page 124)

1. Dust the brisket and short ribs with the flour.
2. Heat the oil in a large skillet. Add the short ribs and brisket
   and brown.
3. In a large saucepan, combine the sausage, salt pork, garlic,
   basil, cumin, thyme, rosemary, celery, onion, salt, and pepper. Add enough beef stock to cover all the ingredients.
4. Boil for 20 minutes, skimming any fat from the top.
5. Preheat the oven to 190°C/375°F/Gas Mark 5.
6. Add the chickpeas to the saucepan.
7. Remove all the ingredients from the saucepan and place in
   a large casserole dish with the short ribs and the brisket.
   Bake for 1 hour and 45 minutes.
8. Put the carrots, sweet potatoes, pumpkin, and corn in the
   saucepan and cook slowly until tender, about 20 minutes.
9. Remove the casserole from the oven, skim any fat from the
   top, and adjust the seasonings as desired. Add the contents
   of the saucepan.
10. Serve over squares of corn bread.

SERVES 10. Serving size: 1 small slice of brisket plus 1 short
rib plus 1 slice of sausage over a 5cm/2in square of corn bread.

Though the meat and chickpea stew known as puchero is widely popular in Spain's Andalusia region and across Spanish-speaking South America, my particular version is inspired by the flavors in the rich Brazilian dish *feijoada*, a pork and black bean soup whose origins can be traced back to the arrival of African slaves on South American shores.

This dish is labor intensive and demands constant attention. However, few dishes will please a crowd more than Puchero and Corn Bread. This stew will serve 10 or more people. If you have more guests, simply add more ingredients—another 450g/1lb of brisket and more frozen corn and 4 more carrots.

Pinto Beans

450g/1lb dried pinto (or borlotti) beans

1 large ham hock

2 garlic cloves, finely chopped

½ medium onion, diced

2 bay leaves

½ teaspoon salt

¼ teaspoon freshly ground pepper

1. Examine the beans, removing any debris, then wash thoroughly. Soak overnight in water to cover.
2. Boil the ham hock for 1½ hours or until tender.
3. Drain the beans.
4. Put the beans, ham hock, and the remaining ingredients in a large saucepan. Bring to a boil.
5. Reduce the heat and simmer for about 1 hour. Remove the bay leaves.
6. Remove 250g/9oz of cooked beans to a large bowl. Mash them with a potato masher until creamy and return to the saucepan. Simmer for another 5 minutes.
7. Serve alone, or with 115g/4oz of rice or a square of corn bread (page 124).

SERVES 4 TO 6. Serving size: 1 cup.

COOKING VEGETARIAN WITH COURAGE I

Even the most eager meat-eater can have a day when she wants vegetables. I had such a day many years ago. I may have had a surfeit of steaks, chops, sausage, and even jerky. I longed for a plate of greens and a bowl of white rice, or I would have been satisfied with a baked potato and a green salad.

I was living in Los Angeles—where the climate is friendly to new trends—and the vegetarian population flourished. One morning, with my appetite calling for steamed rice and broccoli, I found a vegetarian restaurant called Ye Olde Health Food Diner. Once I had settled in, I gave the waitress my order. "Rice and veggies, please."

At the time I was a smoker, and while I am not proud of that statement, I am happy to report that I have been free of nicotine for over twenty years. But I was a smoker when I entered the restaurant on the day in point. After the waitress took my order, I reached into my purse and took out an unopened pack of cigarettes. I don't know if the rustling of the cigarette paper alerted her or if she had a natural alarm for tobacco, but in seconds she turned and raced back to my table. She bent low and brought her face uncomfortably close to mine. She hissed, "Don't you dare. That is a nasty habit." She added, "Filthy, filthy, filthy." I backed up as far as I could in the booth. Her frown would have frightened a dragon. She said, "You have endangered everybody in this place." Mind you, I had not even pulled the little strand of cellophane from the package.

I looked at the customers at the counter, the tables, and in the other booths and they all looked pitiful, and pale. They had long faces, lank hair, sad, half-dead eyes. I said to the waitress, "I suppose these are all newcomers. They just started coming here to get better."

She drew herself up in a huff and responded, "No, these are vegetarians, they have been coming here for years."

I beckoned to her to come close and I hissed into her ear in a stage whisper, "Don't ever tell anyone that these people have been coming here for years, and are still looking no better than they do now."

My statement made her look at her customers, and in that second, I gathered my purse and my unopened cigarettes and fled the joint. I went home and in self-defense I wrote the following poem:

THE HEALTH-FOOD DINER

No sprouted wheat and soya shoots
And brussels in a cake,
Carrot straw and spinach raw
(Today I need a steak).

Not thick brown rice and rice pilau
Or mushrooms creamed on toast,
Turnips mashed and parsnips hashed
(I'm dreaming of a roast).

Health-food folks around the world
Are thinned by anxious zeal,
They look for help in seafood kelp
(I count on breaded veal).

No Smoking signs, raw mustard greens,
Zucchini by the ton,
Uncooked kale and bodies frail
Are sure to make me run

to

Loins of pork and chicken thighs
And standing rib, so prime,
Pork chops brown and fresh ground round
(I crave them all the time).

Irish stews and boiled corned beef
And hot dogs by the scores,
Or any place that saves a space
For smoking carnivores.

Those sentiments of twenty years ago have given way to my becoming enchanted with vegetables.

I have met and adopted two composers and songwriters, Nick Ashford, who is a strict vegetarian, and his wife, Valerie Simpson, who wavers a bit. I love to cook for them, for they are good food lovers with great palates. I have developed a large number of vegetable dishes for them, which I also love. I have discovered that many of these dishes stand shoulder to hip with meat entrees without shyness or apology. I offer a number of them to you in the pages that follow.

Omelet with Spinach

1. Oil a 20 × 11cm/8 × 4½-in loaf pan. Set aside.
2. Heat the tomatoes in 1 tablespoon of the olive oil in a large skillet until the liquid has mostly evaporated.
3. Season with the thyme, salt, and pepper and set aside to cool.
4. Heat the remaining olive oil in a small skillet or saucepan and stir in the spinach. Season to taste with nutmeg.
5. Preheat the oven to 200°C/400°F/Gas Mark 6.
6. Break the eggs into a large bowl and beat with an electric mixer.
7. Add the cream and the cheese.
8. Mix the tomatoes and the spinach together and place them in the bottom of the prepared loaf pan. Pour the egg mixture on top.
9. Place the loaf pan in a larger pan half-filled with hot water and place the larger pan in the oven.
10. Bake for 35 to 45 minutes, until the omelet is puffed and lightly golden.
11. Remove the loaf pan from the oven by itself. Run a knife around the edges of the pan to loosen the omelet, and invert the omelet onto a plate. Reinvert the omelet onto a serving platter.
12. Serve hot or at room temperature with a green salad tossed with olives and a bit of olive oil. This omelet will also work well as a sandwich filling.

SERVES 4. Serving size: ¼ omelet.

800g/1¾lb can whole plum tomatoes, chopped
1½ tablespoons olive oil
¼ teaspoon dried thyme
½ teaspoon salt
¼ teaspoon pepper
175g/6oz cooked spinach
Freshly grated nutmeg
4 large eggs
2 tablespoons heavy (double) cream
50g/2oz Gruyère cheese, grated

Baked Eggs

4 large eggs

½ large onion, thickly sliced

50g/2oz butter, melted

325ml/11floz milk

4 teaspoons fresh lemon
   juice

4 teaspoons chopped fresh
   parsley

½ teaspoon curry powder

¼ teaspoon ground cumin

⅛ teaspoon red pepper
   flakes (or fresh red pepper)

75g/3oz Swiss cheese,
   grated

40g/1½oz cheddar cheese,
   grated

1. Hard-boil the eggs and remove the shells. Put the eggs back in their water to keep warm.
2. Sauté the onion in the butter in a large skillet for 10 to 12 minutes, until just tender.
3. Pick up the onion in a slotted spoon and remove to paper towels to drain, reserving the drippings for a later use, if desired.
4. Slice the eggs into halves and place, yolks up, in a baking dish.
5. Preheat the oven to 180°C/350°F/Gas Mark 4.
6. Mix the onion with the milk, 2 tablespoons water, the lemon juice, parsley, curry powder, cumin, red pepper flakes, and cheeses in a large bowl. Pour around the eggs.
7. Place the baking dish in the oven and bake for 30 minutes.

SERVES 4. Serving size: 1 egg with 1 serving of green salad. (Remember, you can go back in a few hours for seconds.)

Thousand Island Eggs

115g/4oz sour cream

4 tablespoons chopped stuffed olives

1 tablespoon chopped fresh chives

4 tablespoons tomato ketchup

Pinch of garlic salt

Dash of hot pepper sauce

½ teaspoon salt

¼ teaspoon pepper

4 teaspoons butter

4 eggs

1. Mix together the sour cream, olives, chives, ketchup, garlic salt, hot pepper sauce, salt, and pepper in a medium bowl.
2. Preheat the oven to 200°C/400°F/Gas Mark 6.
3. Put 1 teaspoon butter in each of four ramekins or baking cups, and put the ramekins in the oven to melt the butter quickly.
4. Remove the ramekins, and break 1 raw egg into each (the eggs will begin to cook immediately). Pour the sour cream mixture, evenly divided, over the eggs, and place in the oven. Bake for 15 to 20 minutes, until set.

SERVES 4. Serving size: 1 ramekin.

This dish can be cooled and still enjoyed. Simply warm the egg in a microwave for 30 seconds and serve with a few tablespoons of cooked vegetables or a few thick slices of salted ripe tomatoes drizzled with balsamic vinegar. This dish is excellent for a midnight snack, or early morning breakfast.

TIP

Temperature Control

It is wise to make certain foods to be served hot, some to be served at room temperature, and others whose flavor comes through best when they are ice cold.

When serving a dinner buffet-style, arrange to have hot foods served hot from a chafing dish. Be certain that foods you are serving at room temperature are correctly served that way.

Kasha

1 egg, beaten

150g/5oz kasha (roasted buckwheat)

1 teaspoon salt

50g/2oz vegetable shortening (white vegetable fat)

1. Combine the egg, kasha, and salt in a bowl, mixing thoroughly.
2. Melt the shortening in a large skillet. Stir in the kasha mixture and 475ml/16fl oz water. Bring to a boil, then quickly reduce the heat to low.
3. Cook, tightly covered, over low heat for about 30 minutes or until the grains are soft.
4. Serve as you would rice or vegetables, or in soups, or with gravy.

SERVES 3 OR 4. Serving size: 2 tablespoons.

Succotash

1. Combine the ingredients in a large, heavy pot. Simmer, covered, for about 15 minutes over low heat.
2. Increase the heat and cook for 30 minutes more, stirring occasionally. Serve hot.

SERVES 4. Serving size: about 90g/3½oz succotash as a side dish.

175g/6oz lima beans (fresh, frozen, or canned)

175g/6oz frozen whole kernel corn

50ml/2floz chicken stock

1 tablespoon butter

½ teaspoon sugar

½ teaspoon salt

¼ teaspoon pepper

Pink Beans

700g/1lb 9oz dried pink beans or small red beans

2 tablespoons vegetable oil

1 large Spanish onion, chopped

800g/1¾lb canned crushed tomatoes

3 large garlic cloves, chopped

2 large carrots, peeled and chopped

3 celery stalks, chopped

2 bay leaves

½ teaspoon salt

¼ teaspoon pepper

1. Sort through the beans and remove any debris. Rinse and drain the beans.
2. Combine the beans and 2 litres/3½ pints water in a 5-6 litre/9–11 pint pot. Soak overnight.
3. Heat the oil in a large skillet and sauté the remaining ingredients until the onion is translucent.
4. Drain the beans and add 2 litres/3½ pints water. Bring to a boil, then reduce the heat, cover, and simmer until the beans are tender to the bite, 2 to 2½ hours. Remove bay leaves.
5. Combine beans and vegetables, stirring well. Season to taste with additional salt if needed.

SERVES 8. Serving size: about 175g/6oz of beans with 90g/3½oz cooked white rice.

If made ahead of time, cover and refrigerate. Before serving, bring to a simmer over medium heat, stirring constantly. Serve with white rice and garnish with cilantro (fresh coriander).

Southern-Style Green Beans

1. Remove the tips from the beans and break the beans into pieces 2.5–4cm/1–1½in long.
2. Wash and dry the beans.
3. Heat the canola oil and olive oil in a large skillet. Cook the sliced onion for 3 minutes.
4. Add the green beans, mushrooms, and salt.
5. Cook slowly, covered, for 30 to 40 minutes, until tender. When the beans are done, there should be very little or no liquid left in the skillet.
6. Serve hot as a main dish or as a side dish.

SERVES 2 AS A MAIN DISH, 4 AS A SIDE DISH. Serving size: 150g/5oz as a main dish, 75g/3oz as a side dish.

450g/1lb green beans

1 teaspoon vegetable oil

1 teaspoon olive oil

½ medium onion, sliced

450g/1lb portobello mushrooms, sliced

1 teaspoon salt

California Green Chile and Cheese Pie

1. Preheat the oven to 180°C/350°F/Gas Mark 4. Bake the piecrust just until pale golden, about 12 minutes. Remove from the oven and let cool slightly.
2. Reduce the oven temperature to 160°C/325°F/Gas Mark 3.
3. Sprinkle the Jack cheese and half of the cheddar cheese over the bottom of the partially baked crust.
4. Evenly distribute the chiles over the cheese.
5. Beat together the cream, eggs, and cumin, if using, in a bowl, until blended. Pour over the chiles.
6. Sprinkle evenly with the remaining cheddar cheese.
7. Bake on a baking sheet for 40 minutes or until the center of the pie appears set when the pan is gently shaken. Let stand for about 15 minutes before cutting.
8. Serve warm or at room temperature.

SERVES 6. Serving size: 1 slice.

1 frozen single piecrust

175g/6oz Monterey Jack or Gruyère cheese, grated

115g/4oz mild cheddar cheese, grated

115g/4oz diced green chiles (from a jar or can), drained

250ml/8fl oz half-and-half or light (single) cream

3 large eggs

⅛ teaspoon ground cumin (optional)

This pie can be separated into 6 slices. Served with green salad, it makes a light yet filling supper.

Corn Pudding

1 tablespoon melted butter

850g/1lb 14oz whole kernel corn

4 eggs

120ml/4fl oz half-and-half (single cream)

3 tablespoons all-purpose (plain) flour

½ teaspoon sugar

¼ teaspoon grated nutmeg

¼ teaspoon ground cinnamon

½ teaspoon salt

¼ teaspoon pepper

1. Using the melted butter, grease a medium casserole dish.
2. Drain the corn as completely as possible.
3. Whisk the eggs together briskly in a large bowl, until blended. Add the half-and-half and continue to blend.
4. Preheat the oven to 180°C/350°F/Gas Mark 4.
5. Add the flour, sugar, nutmeg, cinnamon, salt, and pepper to the egg mixture and stir well. Add the corn and mix together.
6. Pour into the prepared casserole dish and bake for 1 hour.
7. Remove from the oven and let cool for 15 minutes. Serve hot as a side dish or as a snack.

SERVES 4 OR 5. Serving size: ½ cup.

Consider the richness of the ingredients. Enjoy a small portion.

COOKING VEGETARIAN
WITH COURAGE II

Hundreds of cookbooks line the walls in my country kitchen. I can sit at the table and reach the books. Since I have read each one at least one time, I do not make a selection. I simply choose whatever book my hand falls on. When I look up, it is to find that my stomach is making unpleasant gurgling sounds, my saliva glands have been hard at work, and two hours have passed.

I rarely follow recipes from one cookbook at a time. I will study three recipes for the same dish to see how three different cooks would prepare the ingredients. I might select ideas from one, and then add my own innovation. The end results are not always successful, but the chances and changes, more often than not, offer a wonderful dish that I doubt any of the original cooks would recognize. Experimenting can breathe new life into vegetable dishes that will satisfy even the most discriminating palates.

Enjoy!

Crudités with Vinaigrette

1. In a large saucepan, boil the potatoes in 1 litre/1¾ pints of salted water until soft, about 20 minutes. Remove the potatoes from the water and set aside.
2. Add the asparagus, broccoli, carrots, peas, and scallions, and boil together for 6 minutes.
3. Remove the vegetables from the pot and rinse in ice water. Drain the vegetables and dry. Peel and cut the potatoes in half, and put them in a large bowl with the other cooked vegetables.
4. Prepare the dressing: In a blender, puree 3 tablespoons cold water, the vinegar, parsley, tarragon, salt, and pepper until smooth.
5. With the motor running, gradually add the olive oil, increasing the flow as the mixture thickens. Turn the blender off and on to mix the ingredients well.
6. Pour 4 tablespoons of dressing over the vegetables in the bowl and mix together.
7. Arrange vegetables and the raw mushrooms on the lettuce leaves in a basket and serve.

SERVES 6 TO 8. Serving size: ½ cup as a side dish, 1 cup as a main dish.

5 small red potatoes

¼ teaspoon salt

225g/8oz asparagus, tough ends snapped off

300g/11oz broccoli, cut into small florets

6 small carrots, peeled

10 edible-pod peas, strings removed

6 scallions (spring onions), including green tops, chopped

225g/8oz small (2.5–4cm/ 1–1½in diameter) button mushroom caps, cleaned with damp towel

4 or 5 small inner leaves from 1 head of romaine lettuce, washed and crisped by soaking in ice water

Dressing

3 tablespoons white wine vinegar

40g/1½oz fresh parsley, chopped

1½ teaspoons dried tarragon, crumbled

½ teaspoon salt

¼ teaspoon pepper

300ml/½ pint olive oil

Pressed Leek, Asparagus, and Zucchini Terrine with Mustard-Lemon Dressing

675g/1½lb small to medium leeks

½ teaspoon dried tarragon

¼ teaspoon salt

350ml/12fl oz vegetable stock (not low-sodium)

450g/1lb zucchini (courgettes), cut into 1cm/½-in slices

450g/1lb asparagus, tough ends snapped off

Mustard-Lemon Dressing

120ml/4fl oz olive oil

3 tablespoons lemon juice

1 tablespoon Dijon mustard

¼ teaspoon pepper

Salt to taste

1. Oil the sides and bottom of a 13 × 23cm/5 × 9-in loaf pan and set aside together with an unoiled loaf pan the same size.
2. Trim the root ends and tops from the leeks (save 10 tender green inner leaves from the tops), leaving about 2.5cm/1in of dark green leaves.
3. Cut the leeks in half lengthwise and rinse under running water, gently separating the layers to remove dirt. Rinse the reserved inner leaves and set the leeks aside.
4. In a 4- to 5-litre/7–9 pint pan, bring the tarragon, salt, and stock to a boil over high heat.
5. Add all the leeks, reduce the heat, cover, and simmer until tender when pierced, about 15 minutes. Remove the leeks from the pan and drain, reserving the cooking water.
6. Add the zucchini and asparagus to the pan and let boil for 4 minutes. Remove and drain.
7. Layer the vegetables in the prepared loaf pan, beginning with the leeks, until all the vegetables are in.
8. Set the other loaf pan on top of the vegetables and fill with 1.8kg/4lb of weight to weigh them down. Canned goods or dried beans work best.
9. Refrigerate for at least 8 hours or up to 2 days to firm.
10. Prepare the dressing: In a blender, combine the olive oil, lemon juice, mustard, pepper, and salt. Refrigerate until ready to use.
11. When ready to serve the terrine, remove from the refrigerator and pour off any liquid that has accumulated. Remove the weighted pan, and with a very sharp knife, gently cut the loaf crosswise into 10 slices.
12. Using two spatulas, lift out the slices to a platter or individual salad plates. (Though more difficult to slice, the terrine is handsome inverted onto a platter. Cut carefully.) Top with the dressing and season with salt.

SERVES 6. **Serving size: 1½ slices.**

Broccoli Piquant

1. Cook the broccoli in a medium skillet according to the package directions.
2. Add the vinegar and garlic to the broccoli, and continue cooking for 10 minutes. Remove the broccoli from the skillet and cut into pieces. Set the broccoli aside.
3. Add the butter to the skillet and heat until melted. Add the breadcrumbs and cook until brown.
4. Pour the breadcrumbs and butter over the hot broccoli and sprinkle with additional crumbs.

SERVES 2 TO 3. Serving size: ½ cup.

275g/10oz frozen broccoli florets (or use steamed fresh broccoli)

2 tablespoons apple cider vinegar

½ garlic clove, finely chopped

1 tablespoon butter

15g/½oz soft breadcrumbs

Roasted Vegetables

1 rutabaga (swede), quartered

2 turnips, halved

1 potato, quartered

3 medium carrots, peeled and halved

4 small white onions, peeled

1 eggplant (aubergine), peeled and quartered lengthwise

1 zucchini (courgette), sliced into 5mm/¼-in rounds

2 yellow squash, sliced into 5mm/¼-in rounds

10 asparagus spears, tough ends snapped off

6 broccoli florets

Seasoning

115g/4oz dried onion soup mix

3 tablespoons extra virgin olive oil

2 tablespoons granulated garlic

1 teaspoon seasoning salt

½ teaspoon fresh ground pepper

1. Grease a large, shallow baking pan.
2. In a large saucepan, bring 1 litre/1¾ pints water to a boil over high heat and add the rutabaga, turnips, potato, carrots, and onions. Boil for 4 minutes.
3. Drain and allow to cool for 30 minutes.
4. Preheat the oven to 180°C/350°F/Gas Mark 4. Slice the onions into 5mm/¼-in-thick disks, but do not separate the rings.
5. While the vegetables are cooling, prepare the seasoning: In a small bowl, whisk together the soup mix, olive oil, garlic, seasoning salt, and pepper.
6. Rub the seasoning over the eggplant, zucchini, squash, asparagus, broccoli, and boiled vegetables, coating completely, and place in the pan. Layer the onion disks on top.
7. Bake for 35 to 40 minutes, until as brown as desired.

SERVES 4. Serving size: 1 piece of each roasted vegetable.

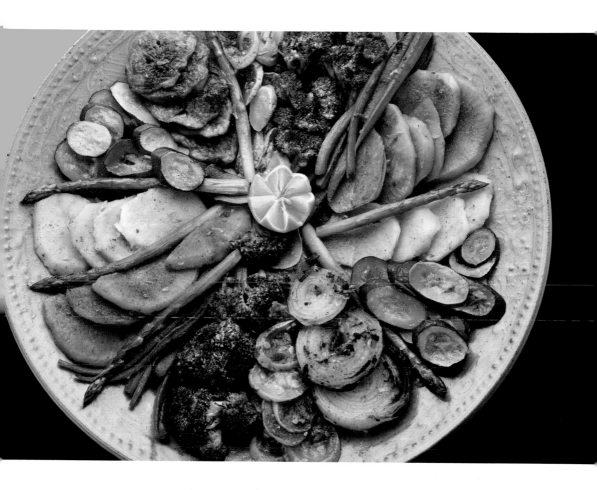

If you let these vegetables come to room temperature, make a vinaigrette of 2 tablespoons olive oil, 1½ tablespoons balsamic vinegar, and 1 tablespoon water. Mix it well and pour it over the roasted vegetables, and you'll have a dish so delicious it will make portion control a difficult task.

Brussels Sprouts and Mushrooms

800g/1¾lb Brussels sprouts (fresh or frozen)

½ teaspoon salt, or more to taste

40g/1½oz butter

225g/8oz white button mushrooms, sliced into 5mm/¼-in pieces

1 medium onion, sliced into 5mm/¼-in pieces

1 green bell pepper, sliced into 5mm/¼-in pieces

¼ teaspoon pepper, or more to taste

1. Wash and trim the sprouts. With a sharp knife make an X in the stem of each sprout.
2. Bring 250ml/8fl oz water to a boil in a saucepan and add the salt. Add the sprouts and cook, uncovered, for 8 to 10 minutes over medium heat until crisp-tender.
3. Drain and place the sprouts in a bowl.
4. Meanwhile, in a large skillet, heat the butter and add the mushrooms, onion, and bell pepper. Cook until tender.
5. Add to the sprouts and season with salt and pepper.

SERVES 4. Serving size: 150g/5oz as a main dish.

Orange-Stuffed Squash

1. Wash the squash and cut into halves lengthwise. Scoop out the seeds.
2. In a large skillet, lay the cut sides in approximately 2.5cm/1in water with ¼ teaspoon salt. Cover and let steam over medium heat for 15 minutes. Drain, pat dry, and remove, cut side up, to a baking dish.
3. Meanwhile, preheat the oven to 200°C/400°F/Gas Mark 6.
4. Put 1 teaspoon brown sugar, 1 generous teaspoon butter, and a pinch of salt in the center of each squash half.
5. Place the baking dish in the oven and bake for 15 minutes.
6. While the squash is baking, combine the remaining brown sugar, the oranges, orange juice, and cinnamon in a bowl.
7. Remove the baking dish, place ½ teaspoon of the orange mixture into each squash half, and return to the oven for another 30 minutes.
8. Turn off the oven. Let sit in the cooling oven for 30 minutes. Serve warm.

SERVES 4. Serving size: ½ squash.

2 acorn squash (about 900g/2lb)

½ teaspoon salt

50g/2oz brown sugar

1½ tablespoons butter or margarine

2 oranges, peeled and segmented

250ml/8fl oz store-bought orange juice

1 teaspoon ground cinnamon

Sweet Potatoes McMillan

1. Preheat the oven to 190°C/375°F/Gas Mark 5. Butter a 1-litre/1¾pint casserole dish. Melt 25g/1oz of butter and set aside.
2. Combine the sweet potatoes, 50g/2oz butter, the sugar, ginger, cinnamon, and salt in a large bowl. Mix well.
3. Stir in the Grand Marnier and milk until fully incorporated.
4. Turn into the prepared casserole dish, brush the top with the melted butter, and sprinkle with the orange zest–sugar mix.
5. Bake for 30 to 40 minutes, until browned.

SERVES 6. Serving size: 2 tablespoons.

Some hosts serve this as a side dish with roasted fresh ham or roasted pork.

75g/3oz butter or margarine, plus more for pan

1kg/2¼lb mashed boiled (with skin on) sweet potatoes

50g/2oz sugar

¼ teaspoon ground ginger

½ teaspoon ground cinnamon

¼ teaspoon salt

50ml/2floz Grand Marnier

2 tablespoons milk or light (single) cream

1 tablespoon grated orange zest mixed with 1 tablespoon sugar

A PINT OF SOUP

unt Tee (T for Teresa) was known to be an excellent and generous cook who liked a glass of whiskey from time to time. She used a ploy that rarely failed because she didn't use it too often.

She told me she would cut up an onion and two cloves of garlic and put them in water to boil. When one of her friends came by, she would open the kitchen door and let the aroma invade the living room. The visitor would ask, "What are you cooking, Tee?" Her answer would be "A little bit of this and a little bit of that. But, you know, I am fresh out of bourbon."

That would be the cue for the man to say "I'll go get a pint."

In his absence, Aunt Tee would turn off the pot and close the door. She would bring glasses and ice with her to the cocktail table. The visitor, whose tongue would be dripping at the prospect of a "Teresa meal," would be told, "That pot in there"—pointing to the kitchen—"is preparation for something I am cooking tomorrow."

People in the family laughed at that story for generations. But I did learn that if I was lonely, or had been away from my home for two or three weeks, my house needed the fix of some aromatic promises coming from my kitchen.

I have gone to the stove, without expecting any visitors, and needing no one to bring me whiskey, and whipped up a beef bourguignonne, chicken and dumplings, or just bacon and eggs.

A lonely house—cold and unfriendly, not necessarily in temperature, but in aloofness—is a place offering scant welcome even to its owner.

The kitchen, which may be floor-licking clean, does not promise the passerby delicious concoctions.

When I return home after being away, I follow an unchanging routine that warms my house and makes it happy to have me back. I open the front door, put my luggage down inside, and immediately go to the kitchen. I take an onion and a potato from the pantry. I wash the potato, and peel and slice each vegetable. I put a heavy-bottomed skillet on the stove with one tablespoon vegetable oil and turn the fire to a medium heat. As it heats, I add the sliced vegetables. I don't want to fry them, so I turn down the heat. I add one clove of minced garlic, a package of frozen mixed vegetables, two bay leaves, and two cups of beef stock. I cover the skillet and turn the fire to its lowest number.

Then I take the luggage to the bedroom and leave the door open. As the aromas begin to reach down the hall, I can almost hear the walls and floorboards and carpet hum in preparation for singing a Welcome Home composition.

In the kitchen I remove the cover and let the warm aromatic steam gush forth, moistening my face, neck, and arms. When I have dried myself, I look around. My house is mine again. It is no longer angry with me for leaving it so long, alone so long. I never know exactly what I shall do with the skillet of vegetables, whether it will become a soup, a stew, or just pureed stock for future use.

All I know is my house has forgiven me and taken me safely back into its loving care.

Try this ploy: Whenever the house resists you, the kitchen can be made into your ally. Start there first, and start with soup.

Black Bean Soup

1. Examine the beans, removing any debris, then wash. Soak overnight in cold water to cover.
2. Drain the beans. In a soup kettle or pot put 1 litre/1¾ pints of stock, the beans, onions, garlic, ham hock if desired, salt, and pepper.
3. Bring to a boil, then turn the heat down and simmer for about 2 hours, until the beans are very soft and the ham hock, if using, is tender.
4. Remove the skin and bones from the ham hock and place the hock in a blender with 2 to 3 cupfuls of beans. Blend until smooth. Repeat until all the beans are pureed.
5. Return the bean puree to the pot and simmer for 5 minutes over low heat. Thin with stock or water if necessary.
6. Serve hot, with a dollop of sour cream atop the soup in each bowl. Reheat as a snack anytime.

SERVES 6 TO 8. Serving size: 250ml/8fl oz.

450g/1lb dried black beans

3 litres/5½ pints chicken stock (or vegetable stock if preferred, or water)

1½ medium onions, chopped

1 garlic clove, chopped

1 ham hock (optional)

¼ teaspoon salt

¼ teaspoon pepper

225g/8oz sour cream

Chicken Soup

1. Heat the oil in a large skillet. Add the chicken and cook well over medium heat.
2. Combine the chicken, chicken stock, and lemon juice in a large saucepan. Add the salt and pepper and simmer for 20 minutes.
3. Add the zucchini, squash, green beans, and asparagus. Cook for 20 minutes.

SERVES 4. Serving size: 250ml/8fl oz.

One steaming bowl of chicken soup will be a wonderful way to break your fast in the morning. Also, roasted vegetables (page 96) work deliciously in this soup. Use them in place of the zucchini, squash, green beans, and asparagus.

1½ tablespoons vegetable oil

150g/5oz skinless chicken, diced

1 litre/1¾ pints chicken stock

⅔ teaspoon lemon juice

⅓ teaspoon salt

¼ teaspoon pepper

40g/1½oz zucchini (courgette), diced

40g/1½oz yellow squash, diced

40g/1½oz green beans, diced

40g/1½oz asparagus, diced

Pumpkin Soup I

25g/1oz butter

2 tablespoons all-purpose
(plain) flour

600ml/1pint milk

¼ teaspoon ground
cinnamon

¼ teaspoon ground nutmeg

½ teaspoon salt

50g/2oz brown sugar

500g/1¼lb canned pumpkin
puree

1 litre/1¾ pints vegetable
stock

2 egg yolks, beaten

1. Melt the butter in a large saucepan.
2. Blend in the flour, using a whisk.
3. Over low heat, slowly add the milk, a little at a time, stirring
   constantly until the mixture is a smooth sauce.
4. Combine the cinnamon, nutmeg, salt, brown sugar, and
   pumpkin in a large bowl. Mix well and add to the saucepan.
5. Add the vegetable stock and simmer for 5 minutes.
6. Temper the eggs by pouring a little of the hot liquid into
   them. Mix well and pour the eggs into the soup. Simmer for
   5 minutes.

SERVES 6. Serving size: 1 bowl.

Pumpkin Soup II

1. Preheat the oven to 180°C/350°F/Gas Mark 4.
2. Split the pumpkin in half. Remove the seeds and save them.
3. Put both pumpkin halves, cut side down, in a deep roasting pan with 1cm/½in of water. Bake for 40 minutes.
4. While the pumpkin is cooking, thoroughly wash the seeds. Pat dry and sprinkle with salt. Toast the seeds in the vegetable oil in a hot skillet and set aside.
5. Remove the pumpkin from the oven and let cool. When cool enough to handle, scoop out the flesh into a large bowl; you need about 500g/1¼lb. Freeze any leftovers in 4 portions for use later.
6. Put the milk, vegetable stock, and pumpkin in a medium saucepan and heat, mixing thoroughly, until all the ingredients are blended.
7. Serve hot. Sprinkle on the cinnamon and to each bowl add a spoonful of sour cream and a few sprinkles of toasted seeds.

SERVES 4. Serving size: 250ml/8fl oz.

1 large pumpkin (about 1.3kg/3lb)
Salt
2 tablespoons vegetable oil
300ml/½ pint milk
475ml/16fl oz vegetable stock
¼ teaspoon ground cinnamon
225g/8oz sour cream

I often make this soup from scratch during October, when pumpkins are available everywhere.

Consommé Double

2 litres/3½ pints chicken stock

1 medium onion, diced

2 celery stalks

3 garlic cloves

2 bay leaves

Chicken backs and necks, fresh or frozen

1. Fill a generous pot with the chicken stock and 1 litre/1¾ pints water. Add the onion, celery, garlic, and bay leaves. Boil for 20 to 25 minutes.
2. Put the pieces of chicken, fresh or frozen, into the stock. Boil vigorously for 1 hour.
3. Take the pot off the stove and let the contents cool.
4. Skim off any scum at the top, then strain the broth. (I pour it through a four-ply cheesecloth in a strainer.)
5. Place the strained broth in the freezer in 6 small packets (350ml/12fl oz per packet) so the entire batch does not have to be defrosted.

SERVES 6. Serving size: 1 cup.

This broth is made even better if you can use the frozen necks, gizzards, and livers from turkeys that you have roasted. Because we are starting with chicken stock instead of water and making the stock much stronger by cooking it with pieces of poultry, the broth is called a consommé double.

TIP

Refrigerator Soup

When I want to warm up my house, perk up my personality, and most in general give myself a feeling of good time, I have often gone to my refrigerator and made a refrigerator soup.

The ingredients are a compilation of anything edible that will fit into a pot and will go with my frozen poultry stock.

A pot of aromatic soup is great ammunition against depression.

THIS WINTER DAY

The kitchen is its readiness
white green and orange things
leak their blood selves in the soup.

Ritual sacrifice that snaps
an odor at my nose and starts
my tongue to march,
slipping in the liquid of its drip.

The day, silver striped
in rain, is balked against
my window and the soup.

OUR DAILY BREAD

tolen waters are sweet, and bread eaten in secret is pleasant." So we are told in the Book of Proverbs in the King James Version of the Holy Bible. I know that bread eaten in secret can be wonderful. But if you eat enough, it will be a secret no longer.

I had a family member who was gentle and soft-spoken, with the patience of Job. However, if his wife set the table without putting bread on it, he lost his pretty ways. He would shout, knock the table, and stomp his feet until she placated him with a pan of biscuits, a skillet of corn bread, or a sliced loaf of white bread.

In Proverbs 23:2, we are advised to ". . . put a knife to thy throat if thou be a person given to appetite." I do not quite agree that one has to be quite so harsh, but I do know that if you want to be svelte and remain that way, control your appetite in the eating of bread. So, I would advise you to eat one piece of bread with the first serving of a dish, and none when you go back for snacks.

Popovers

1. Preheat the oven to 220°C/425°F/Gas Mark 7. Grease six custard cups or an iron popover pan.
2. Beat the eggs slightly in a large bowl.
3. Add the milk and butter, then add the flour and salt. Beat vigorously for 2 minutes.
4. Pour the batter into very hot custard cups or popover pan, filling two-thirds full. Place in the oven and bake for about 40 minutes or until fully risen and brown.
5. Serve at once.

SERVES 6. Serving size: 1 popover with omelet, or 2 plain popovers.

2 eggs

250ml/8fl oz milk

25g/1oz butter, melted

115g/4oz sifted all-purpose (plain) flour

¼ teaspoon salt

If you plan to serve the popovers later, open each popover, place a little savory ham omelet inside, and reheat.

TIP

Biscuit Quick

When making homemade biscuits, I sift all my dry ingredients together, and then cut the shortening (fat) into the mix until it resembles coarse cornmeal. I put it into a zippered bag and into the freezer, where it can stay for up to one year.

When I'm ready to serve biscuits, I take out half of the dry mixture and add 250ml/8fl oz of milk. I roll it on a floured board and cut out biscuits as I desire.

This tip has saved me a lot of time and some anxiety about getting flour on my clothes, or on my face, or on the floor just as I am about to serve.

Buttermilk Biscuits

From *Hallelujah! The Welcome Table*

450g/1lb all-purpose (plain) flour

½ teaspoon salt

6 teaspoons baking powder

1 teaspoon baking soda (bicarbonate of soda)

175g/6oz lard

475ml/16fl oz buttermilk

All-purpose flour for sprinkling

1. Preheat the oven to 190°C/375°F/Gas Mark 5.
2. Sift the flour with the salt, baking powder, and baking soda. Cut in the lard until the mixture resembles coarse cornmeal. Add the buttermilk, and stir until the dough leaves the sides of the bowl.
3. Turn the dough out onto a lightly floured board and knead until smooth. Roll out to a 1cm/½-in thickness and cut into 5cm/2-in rounds. If there is no biscuit cutter at hand, use a water glass. (Turn glass upside down, dust rim in flour, and cut biscuits.)
4. Bake on an ungreased cookie sheet for 20 to 25 minutes, until the biscuits are golden brown.

MAKES 2 DOZEN BISCUITS

Serving size: 1 biscuit

Orange Nut Bread

1. Grease a 23 × 13 × 7.5cm/9 × 5 × 3-in loaf pan with shortening.
2. Sift the flour, baking powder, salt, and sugar into a large bowl.
3. Cut in the shortening with a pastry blender, two knives, or your fingers until the ingredients are about the size of green peas.
4. Add the milk, orange juice, and egg, mixing only enough to dampen the flour mixture.
5. Stir in the grated rind and nuts, being careful not to over-mix.
6. Pour into the prepared loaf pan, spreading the batter to the corners and leaving a slight depression in the center. Let stand for 20 minutes.
7. Meanwhile, preheat the oven to 180°C/350°F/Gas Mark 4.
8. Bake for about 1 hour or until the top is golden and a knife inserted into the center of the bread comes out clean.
9. Let stand for 5 minutes, then invert onto a rack to cool.
10. Store overnight in the icebox before slicing.

SERVES 8. Serving size: 1 slice.

50g/2oz vegetable shortening (white vegetable fat), plus more for pan

275g/10oz all-purpose (plain) flour

2 teaspoons baking powder

½ teaspoon salt

200g/7oz sugar

175ml/6fl oz milk

50ml/2fl oz fresh orange juice

1 egg

1 tablespoon grated orange rind

115g/4oz chopped nuts

Enjoy with tea or coffee at any time, day or night.

Corn Sticks

50ml/2fl oz melted shortening or vegetable oil, plus more for pans

50g/2oz all-purpose (plain) flour

115g/4oz yellow cornmeal

1 teaspoon baking powder

½ teaspoon salt

1 teaspoon sugar

1 egg, beaten

120ml/4fl oz milk

Serve with mixed green salad or as a snack with a bowl of hot chicken broth. Enjoy one!

1. Preheat the oven to 230°C/450°F/Gas Mark 8. Grease cast iron corn stick or muffin pans.
2. Sift together the flour, cornmeal, baking powder, salt, and sugar.
3. Add the egg, milk, and melted shortening or oil, stirring until just blended. Mix only enough to dampen the corn-meal mixture.
4. Heat the greased corn stick pans in the oven for 20 minutes.
5. Pour in the batter and bake for about 30 minutes or until done and beautifully brown. Pierce 1 corn stick with a toothpick. If toothpick comes out clean, the bread is done.

SERVES 4. Serving size: 1 corn stick.

Orange Syrup for Waffles, Pancakes, or Toast

475ml/16fl oz orange juice
175g/6oz honey
25g/1oz butter

1. Boil the orange juice in a medium saucepan and reduce it to 250ml/8fl oz.
2. Add the honey and butter. Stir well until all the ingredients are blended.
3. Pour over pancakes, griddle cakes, waffles, or pastries for a company-pleasing trimming.

Makes about 350ml/12fl oz.

All Day and All Night Corn Bread

3 tablespoons butter

50g/2oz all-purpose (plain) flour

175g/6oz white cornmeal

2 tablespoons sugar

1 teaspoon salt

1 tablespoon baking powder

375ml/13fl oz milk

1 egg, well beaten

When the corn bread has cooled, a 5cm/2in square can be removed. Open the square horizontally so there is a top and a bottom. Put in one slice of Swiss cheese or Monterey Jack cheese and warm in a toaster oven. Serve for breakfast with the hot beverage of your choice.

1. Preheat the oven to 200°C/400°F/Gas Mark 6. Melt the butter in a 20cm/8in square pan.
2. Sift together the flour, cornmeal, sugar, salt, and baking powder into a large bowl.
3. Stir in 280ml/9fl oz of the milk and the egg, mixing only enough to dampen the cornmeal mixture.
4. Pour the batter into the pan. Pour the remaining milk over the batter and stir.
5. Bake for 35 to 45 minutes, until the top is golden and a toothpick inserted into the center of the bread comes out clean.

SERVES 9. Serving size: 1 square.

LETTUCE PRAISE SALADS

The Presiding Elder—his title is spoken of in ALL CAPS—is, in the Methodist Church, a man of great stature, whether he is a six-footer with great confidence and a booming voice or he is a short roly-poly person with charming ways and a melodious voice.

In Arkansas, where I was growing up under the care of my loving paternal grandmother and her other son, my Uncle Willie, the Presiding Elder's visit was heralded almost as a holiday, no matter that such visits were part of his formal responsibilities, to be done once every three months at each of the churches under his charge. He would preach a fiery sermon, go over the books with the church trustees and preacher, give pep talks to the usher board, and have a glorious scrumptious dinner, always cooked by my grandmother. It was on one of his visits that I began a lifelong love affair with salad.

One Sunday morning, the Presiding Elder had preached until you could smell the very embers of hell burning for those who had disobeyed the church teachings. And those who had been obedient servants could hear the bell-like sounds of the angels' choir—singing "Welcome home, welcome, Christians. You have done well. Welcome, welcome to the Golden Streets of Heaven; you have done well!" Anyway, all of the adults were under his spell, but the children had to use incredible control to keep from laughing at his lugubrious speech and his large unattractive belly.

For the dinner following this sermon, my grandmother had cooked a ham and some large fluffy biscuits and fried a chicken to its golden promising end. She had made a potato salad, and to decorate the dish, she halved more hard-boiled eggs than usual and placed some of them on top, pushing many more down into the salad.

We grew lettuce, which never formed a ball; its leaves were wide, flat, and tender. I had washed the lettuce and my brother Bailey had crushed ice and we put it into my grandmother's crystal bowl. The common way of eating potato salad showed a diner laying one leaf of lettuce onto a salad plate. Then one to two spoons of potato salad would be placed in the center of the salad leaf.

That particular Sunday, the Presiding Elder blessed the table and I thought that he thought he was again in the pulpit, preaching another long-winded sermon. I peeked out of half-closed eyes and saw the ham fat had turned white on the platter and my grandmother's beautiful biscuits, so fluffy earlier, had sat down on themselves. When he finally finished saying the blessing, he looked over the chicken and took two of the largest pieces. He chose the thickest slab of ham, and then he attacked the potato salad. He raked about four halves of the eggs on top and then put a mound of potato salad on the plate, which was already about to collapse.

Bailey saw that—in fact, we all saw that—but Bailey was first. He took the fork from the salad bowl and instead of taking one leaf of lettuce, he put the fork down until he reached the bottom of the bowl and he picked up every leaf and shook them and put them all on his plate. My grandmother looked at him and at his action and said nothing. My Uncle Willie said nothing. The preacher was already eating.

Bailey looked at me; I was mute with fear, so he took the fork and started to put the lettuce back into the bowl. My grandmother in her soft, firm voice said, "No, little mister, you will eat every one of those leaves." Bailey looked at me again and he raked off one leaf into his lap and rolled it as if it was a cigarette under the table and gave it to me to eat, raked another, rolled it, and ate it. Each time Bailey reached for a piece of chicken, my grandmother said, "No, little mister, finish your lettuce first." He and I ate every shred of lettuce and my grandmother excused us from the table. We cried and laughed. We were angry and tickled.

When the Presiding Elder had left, my grandmother called Bailey and me back to the dining room. She said, "You know there is always something in the kitchen for Grandmother and her children. I would never let that greedy vulture eat everything. You also must know, for every action you also must pay. Now look in the icebox and bring that salad out here."

Warm Garden Salad

1. Blanch the broccoli, asparagus, leeks, rutabaga, mushrooms, and zucchini in boiling water for 5 minutes. Drain and set aside, keeping warm.
2. Prepare the vinaigrette: In a blender, combine the garlic, vinegar, olive oil, sherry, and mustard. Add salt and pepper to taste and puree.
3. Moisten the vegetables with the vinaigrette and arrange on top of the salad greens.

SERVES 6. Serving size: 1 or 2 pieces of each vegetable on a bed of greens.

8 small broccoli florets

8 asparagus tips

4 small leeks, washed thoroughly

1 small rutabaga (swede), cut into thin strips

2 portobello mushrooms, thinly sliced

2 zucchini (courgettes), thinly sliced

150g/5oz assorted salad greens or 6 romaine lettuce leaves

Vinaigrette

1 garlic clove, crushed

150ml/5fl oz apple cider vinegar

75ml/2½fl oz olive oil

2 tablespoons sherry

¾ teaspoon prepared mustard (any kind will do)

Salt and pepper

You can return to this dish as often as you choose.

Cold Potato Salad

From *Hallelujah! The Welcome Table*

900g/2lb potatoes, cooked,
  peeled and diced

1 medium onion, finely chopped

115g/4oz celery, finely diced

115g/4oz dill pickles (gherkins), chopped

225g/8oz sweet relish, drained

8 large hard-boiled eggs,
  4 chopped, 4 whole

Salt and black pepper

350g/12oz mayonnaise

Fresh parsley, chopped

1. Combine the potatoes, onion, celery, pickles, relish, and chopped eggs. Season with salt and pepper, and add the mayonnaise. Chill for several hours.
2. Just before serving, halve the remaining 4 eggs and place them on the salad as decoration. Dust the salad with chopped parsley and serve at once.

SERVES 6 TO 8

Serving size: 2 heaping tablespoons.

Chicken-and-Pineapple Salad

1. Dice the chicken and pineapple into large pieces.
2. Stir the vinegar, sugar, and mayonnaise together in a large bowl until the sugar is dissolved. Add the chicken and pineapple.
3. Add the mint to taste and stir well. Serve atop lettuce leaves and sprinkle cashews over the salad, if desired.

SERVES 4 OR 5. Serving size: 2 heaping tablespoons.

2 cooked, skinned chicken breasts

4 slices ripe pineapple

120ml/4fl oz rice vinegar or white wine vinegar

2 tablespoons sugar

115g/4oz mayonnaise

Fresh mint, chopped

Lettuce leaves, crisped by soaking in ice water

65g/2½oz cashew nuts, broken, toasted (optional)

Fruit Mélange

225g/8oz canned pitted dark sweet cherries (water packed), drained

200g/7oz fresh strawberries

1 cantaloupe melon, cut into balls (about 450g/1lb)

250g/9oz pineapple chunks, drained

150g/5oz low-sugar orange marmalade

3 teaspoons finely chopped candied ginger

½ ripe banana, sliced

6 fresh mint leaves

1. Chill a large glass serving bowl.
2. Layer the fruit in the chilled bowl, beginning with the cherries and moving on to the strawberries, cantaloupe, and pineapple.
3. In a separate bowl, combine the orange marmalade, 50ml/2fl oz hot water, and the candied ginger to create a sauce.
4. Drizzle the orange marmalade sauce over the fruit and chill for 2 hours before serving.
5. When ready to serve, arrange the banana slices on top of the fruit and garnish with the mint leaves.

SERVES 6. Serving size: 200g/7oz.

To keep the banana from darkening, dip in lemon juice mixed with a little water.

Corn Salad

Combine all the ingredients in a large bowl.

SERVES 6. Serving size: ½ cup.

75g/3oz red pepper, diced

1 roasted green bell pepper, peeled, seeded, and diced

5 green scallion (spring onion) tops, chopped

1 fresh tomato, seeded, finely diced, and squeezed

50ml/2fl oz fresh lemon juice

1 tablespoon extra virgin olive oil

400g/14oz can chickpeas, drained and rinsed

400g/14oz frozen corn, blanched in simmering water for 3 minutes, drained, then immersed in ice water and drained

1 tablespoon honey mustard

½ teaspoon salt

¼ teaspoon pepper

Chicken-and-Peaches Salad

2 boneless, skinless chicken breasts, cooked and chilled

75g/3oz Neufchâtel or cream cheese, at room temperature

4 tablespoons mayonnaise

1 teaspoon chopped fresh basil leaves

½ teaspoon salt

¼ teaspoon white pepper

450g/1lb canned peach halves (juice packed), drained and diced

65g/2½oz cashews, broken, toasted

50g/2oz celery, chopped

4 lettuce leaves

1. Cube the chicken.
2. Combine the cheese, mayonnaise, basil, salt, and pepper in a large bowl.
3. Add the chicken, peaches, cashews, and celery, and toss well.
4. Chill in the refrigerator for 1 hour. When ready to serve, spoon the salad onto the lettuce leaves.

SERVES 4. Serving size: 2 heaping tablespoons.

If you are eating alone, eat sparingly and return to the salad as frequently as you desire.

SWEET ENDINGS

If you find honey, eat just enough.

—*Proverbs 25:16*

Whether speaking of honey or butter or ice cream, or anything, it is wise to eat just enough. You are going to be overjoyed when you manage your portions—even if just for two weeks.

Crème Caramel

1. Scald the milk with the vanilla in a large saucepan over low heat. Remove from the heat and let sit, covered, for 30 minutes.
2. In a separate saucepan, prepare caramel for a 2-litre/3½ pint mold: Combine 3 tablespoons water, the lemon juice, and 115g/4oz sugar and cook over medium-high heat until golden. Watch carefully that it doesn't become too dark and burn, as it may taste bitter.
3. Carefully pour the caramel into the mold, tilting the mold to fully coat the bottom and sides. Let sit until the caramel hardens, about 2 minutes.
4. Preheat the oven to 150°C/300°F/Gas Mark 2.
5. Whisk together the eggs, yolks, the remaining 200g/7oz sugar, and the salt in a large bowl until the mixture is pale yellow and thick enough to coat a spoon or spatula.
6. Pour the scalded milk mixture into the egg mixture and mix well with a wooden spoon to make a custard.
7. Using a fine metal kitchen strainer, carefully strain the custard mixture into the caramelized mold.
8. Place the mold in a larger pan more than 5cm/2in deep. Set the larger pan on an oven shelf, and fill with at least 2.5cm/1in of water, until it comes halfway up the mold.
9. Bake for 60 to 75 minutes, until the custard is set. (You'll know it's ready when a knife inserted in the center comes out clean.) Remove the pan and mold from the oven and set the mold outside the larger pan to cool for 2 hours.
10. Refrigerate for at least 8 hours, or overnight. When ready to serve, run a knife around the edges of the mold. Cover the mold with a deep serving dish and overturn the mold. Allow the caramel to coat the custard. Cut into portions before serving, then serve some of the crème caramel with cream.

SERVES 6. Serving size: 150g/5oz.

1 litre/1¾ pints milk
1 teaspoon pure vanilla extract
⅛ teaspoon lemon juice or vinegar
300g/11oz sugar
8 large eggs
4 large egg yolks
Pinch of salt

The long, slow cooking of this classic dessert produces a perfectly smooth and silky custard.

Pears in Port Wine

4 ripe, firm pears

750ml/1¼pints ruby port wine

50g/2oz sugar

1 jigger (3 tablespoons) Cointreau

2 teaspoons pure vanilla extract

1. Peel the pears, but leave them whole. With the stem end intact, cut off a thin slice at the bottom so that the pears can stand upright.
2. In a nonreactive saucepan, bring the port, sugar, and 475ml/16fl oz water to a boil.
3. Place the whole pears in the liquid, lower the heat, and simmer, uncovered, for about 35 minutes, turning the pears occasionally, until they are tender.
4. Remove the pears with a slotted spoon and set aside to cool.
5. Increase the heat under the saucepan and reduce the liquid by half by boiling vigorously for 20 minutes to a medium-thick syrup. Add the Cointreau and vanilla.
6. Place the pears upright in a serving dish and spoon the reduced syrup over them. Chill for at least 2 hours before serving.

SERVES 4. Serving size: 1 pear, or if half a pear will satisfy, offer vanilla ice cream at the first serving.

Second and third servings could be eaten in the morning with coffee or in the afternoon with a cup of aromatic tea.

TIP

Raise a Glass

White wines such as Chardonnay, Chablis, and Riesling must be served cold. I have not said U.S. wines are the best, but they are my favorites.

Fortunately, there are American wines as tasty as any wine in the world and thankfully less expensive. I serve California, Washington State, and New York wines and have always been pleased with my guests' reception of my choice.

Red wines such as Cabernet Sauvignon, Merlot, Bordeaux, and Pinot Noir are easily found in your local wine store. Some need to be decanted, especially the older, bigger red wines. I encourage you to pour the red wine you are going to serve into a decanter, two hours before dinner, to achieve its optimum flavor.

Some guests still drink sherry. I serve Dry Sack and cocktail sherry before meals and sometimes a good port after dinner. And a generous host provides Grand Marnier, Cointreau, Baileys, Frangelico, and other cognacs and brandies to please the guests.

It must be remembered that a good friend does not allow a guest to drive after too much alcohol. So have a good time and be wise.

Party Hearty

In my early teens, my paternal grandmother brought my brother and me from a dusky little village in Arkansas to live with our mother in San Francisco. The big streets, fast cars, my mother, who wore makeup, and white teachers and students in school frightened me. I wanted to be friendly at least with the other African Americans, but I was too terrified to talk. My fast-talking, brilliant brother made friends immediately, but I closed myself off and became lonelier.

At school, the girls would talk about boys and parties and good times. They did not try to prevent me from hearing them. Finally I went to my mother and told her how lonely I was and that the other girls gave parties where they had fun, but no one invited me. She gave me some advice, which I have used forever. She said, "If someone draws a circle and leaves you out, you draw a bigger circle and include them in it. If they have not invited you to their parties—you invite them to yours."

She encouraged me to go to the five and ten cents store and buy invitations and then write, "Maya invites you to a birthday party. Although it is nobody's birthday that we know, we will have spaghetti with large meatballs, garlic toast of sourdough bread, all the salad you can eat, a massive cake, good music and dancing. Please respond."

I offered ten invitations. Twenty people answered. Some girls brought boys. I was afraid my mother would not want boys and girls in her beautiful house. "They will be all right," she said. "I will cook all the food, Papa Ford will serve buffet style, and I will be here in the house. I will walk through no more than three times. Don't worry—they will behave and you will give a great party."

In my fifties, I moved to North Carolina from California. I already had some fame, but no one invited me to anything, so I had some invitations printed saying, "Maya Angelou invites you to a 'Welcome to Spring Party.' We will have laughter, good food, some dancing, some drinking, and some story-telling." I invited twenty people, remembering what had happened the first time. I prepared for forty and that's how many came. I do not suggest that there are recipes in this book that will help you to make new friends, but I assure you they will introduce you to people you have never heard of.

Happy Cooking and Happy Eating, all day and all night long.

Acknowledgments

I am indebted to Robert Loomis and Porscha Burke of Random House. They demonstrated exquisite patience with me as I slow-crawled through this manuscript.

I am indebted to my late mother for leaving me memories of great food for use all my life long. My indebtedness to M.F.K. Fisher is enormous. From her I learned to be bold in the kitchen but never casual. I learned that the cook may shock but must never be careless.

To Chef Don McMillan and every good cook who dared to serve great tamales, fried chicken, wonton soup, roast beef with Yorkshire pudding, and pasta primavera . . . thank you.

Index

Page references in italic refer to illustrations.